Entrepreneur
VOICES
ON

EFFECTIVE
LEADERSHIP

The Staff of Entrepreneur Media, Inc.

Entrepreneur
PRESS

Entrepreneur Press, Publisher
Cover Design: Andrew Welyczko
Production and Composition: Eliot House Productions

This publication is designed to provide accurate and
authoritative information in regard to the subject matter covered.
It is sold with the understanding that the publisher is not
engaged in rendering legal, accounting or other professional
services. If legal advice or other expert assistance is required, the
services of a competent professional person should be sought.

Library of Congress Cataloging-in-Publication Data
Names: Mintzer, Richard, author. | Entrepreneur Media, Inc.,
    author.
Title: Entrepreneur voices on effective leadership / by The
    Staff of Entrepreneur Media and Rich Mintzer.
Description: Irvine, California: Entrepreneur Media, Inc.,
    [2018] | Series: Entrepreneur voices
Identifiers: LCCN 2017043416| ISBN 978-1-59918-617-7 (alk.
    paper) | ISBN 1-59918-617-9 (alk. paper)
Subjects: LCSH: Leadership.
Classification: LCC HD57.7 .M56 2018 | DDC 658.4/092—dc23
LC record available at https://lccn.loc.gov/2017043416

Printed in the United States of America
22 21 20 19 18   10 9 8 7 6 5 4 3 2 1

CONTENTS

PART II
DEVELOPING LEADERSHIP

PART III

LEADING FROM THE BOTTOM UP

Contents

Contents

FOREWORD BY JEFFREY HAYZLETT

Primetime TV and radio host, former Fortune 100 CMO, and author of **Think Big, Act Bigger**

What is a leader? What makes a good leader? Those are questions we should ask ourselves every day—whether we are currently in a position of power or aspire to be in one. A good leader doesn't just tell others what to do. It's not someone who cracks the whip just because they have power. That's a tyrant—not a leader.

A good leader is someone who guides and mentors their team. They offer counsel and foster a good working environment. They encourage the team to go above and beyond and push them out of their comfort zone in order to achieve great things. A strong leader needs to know their team's capabilities—top to bottom. They should measure their level of success by how their team performs. They must realize that they can only go as fast as their slowest or weakest team member. Even still, authentic leadership involves owning mistakes, setting realistic goals, having a back-up plan (or multiple back-up plans), and being able to meet your conditions of satisfaction, whatever those are. Mine are having fun, making money and growing professionally.

I have been in business for a long time. I have bought and sold over 250 businesses, I have conducted millions of dollars in transactions, and I have seen quite a few changes in leadership over the years. In fact, I recall sitting in a meeting once where everyone was discussing a way to move forward on a project. My boss at the time said we had to move a certain way "because that's the way it's always been." I sat there thinking, "Why are we doing something that's already been done before?"

Doing the same thing over and over while expecting different results is the very definition of insanity. I wanted to speak up and say what was in my mind, but I was young and learning the ropes. *Who wants to hear from the young kid?* Looking back, though, I wish I had spoken up. It might've gotten me a look of disapproval, but it might've also impressed someone else by thinking outside the box.

Being a leader in modern times means letting go of the old way of doing things and accepting that things are different now. In fact, most successful leaders must constantly hold conflicting ideas, choices, possibilities, opportunities, and activities in their heads at the same time. Hence, today's business world requires leaders to be nimble and quickly adapt to fast-moving situations.

Despite the constant change, effective leaders lead. They think big. They come up with great ideas. They fail, they counsel and mentor, and they are part of the team. The most aspiring and successful leaders are in their positions because they aren't afraid to be true to themselves and use that same bravado to represent their brand. I'm a cowboy from South Dakota making my way through the concrete jungle that is New York City, and my personality matches my persona. Authenticity earns leaders respect. After all, no one likes a phony.

By many standards, I have achieved a modicum of success in corporate America. I've been a lobbyist, I've worked in the printing industry, and I've sat in the "corner office" as the Chief Marketing Officer at a Fortune 100 company.

Yet, something was missing.

The entrepreneurial pull was too much for me to ignore. For me, being an entrepreneur is a way of life. I am totally, and constantly, immersed in what I do. It is a life-calling mission—a rush of adrenaline that gets in your system and consumes you . . . in a good way.

As entrepreneurs, we feel the pull to be leaders outside of the restraints set by corporate America. We want to create masterpieces, lead movements, and take action on our own timelines. Sometimes, leading a team can feel like herding cats, but you must find a way to make sure everyone is pulling in the same direction. But embracing the challenges in a way that get everyone aligned is what effective leadership is all about.

Having published *Think Big, Act Bigger* with Entrepreneur, I know firsthand of their mission to address the true needs of current and aspiring entrepreneurs—and current and aspiring leaders—in the ever-changing business world of today.

For the first installment of their *Entrepreneur Voices* series *on Effective Leadership*, they have gathered a vast collection of authors whose experiences have made them thought leaders in their respective fields. Their wide range of knowledge and practical, everyday advice is something that everyone can use—personally and professionally.

Are you ready to take the necessary risks to be a good leader? As I always say to my staff, no one's going to die. Leaders can't be afraid to fail. Leaders need to be irrational, push boundaries, and at times, create tension. Leadership isn't about having power; it's about reaching a diverse number of people and keeping them focused on one goal: moving the company forward!

THE EMERGENCE OF LEADERS

There has long been a debate as to whether leaders are born or made. After numerous surveys and discussions on the topic, there are arguments for both. It is safe to say that most studies find that there are leadership characteristics inherent in some people that make them more likely to excel in such a role. However, training and honing numerous teachable skills create most leaders. It is also worth considering a third factor, and that is the wide range of personal life experiences that leaders use in their roles.

Successful leaders take a variety of paths to leadership. Some highly successful leaders, such as Jack Welch or Sheryl Sandberg, wanted to be at the helm from the start of their careers (or even before). They were often founders or co-founders of businesses that they are now leading. They had a passion, and by sharing, introducing, and enlightening others to what they were passionate about, they were able to become leaders. Others bought into the vision of a company and worked hard to attain a leadership role. Some people trained and honed their leadership skills prior to joining a company. These are the people who were on a path to leadership before even having people to lead. Many of these folks had leadership roles in other aspects of life, from schools to Boy/Girl Scouts to clubs, associations, athletics, or the military.

At the other end of the spectrum, you'll find those who landed in leadership positions by default—no one else wanted the job or was qualified. These are very often people who excelled at their role in the company and there was no place for them to go but up. They became leaders and (often much to their surprise) had to start learning the role on the job and and while still doing their other work. Some make a smooth transition, but most do not unless they understand early that there is a lot to learn.

If you take the time to ask leaders how they landed in a leadership role, they will each have their own unique story. Truth is there is no single path to leadership and certainly no tried-and-true path to leadership success. This is largely because leadership is a "people-skill," and understanding human behavior is no simple task, especially when you take into consideration the culture, background, and personal experiences each person brings with them. Someone can establish policies, set goals, create meeting agendas, and institute all sorts of milestones, but there is more to leadership than meets the eye.

Albert Einstein said, "Not everything that counts can be counted, and not everything that can be counted counts." This is appropriate when it comes to great leadership. Even in a world of, Quick Ratios, KPIs, ROIs, NOPATs, EBITs, and cash flow management, neither the numbers nor the technology can replace the human factor, which is the most significant quality of most great leaders. Whether it's running a mom and pop shop or a multinational conglomerate, a great leader will need to possess skills and characteristics that may not always be measurable. This includes communication (and listening) skills, plus the ability to be fair and open-minded, able to diffuse crisis situations, have difficult conversations, and empower other people.

The upcoming pages feature many of *Entrepreneur*'s articles on the topic of leadership. They list and explain many of the traits, attributes, and characteristics that great leaders possess. There are examples of various leadership situations and many how-to recommendations. Perhaps the overwhelming theme is simply this: be a good person to other people, and you will be rewarded. After all, leaders are best rewarded when those who they are leading succeed.

As you proceed, you will inevitably recognize some attributes and characteristics that you already possess. You will also see others that you may need to focus on more closely. You may want to take some notes as you go forward and even reread the articles that inspire you the most. There are volumes written on leadership, but in a fast-paced world, this is the abridged version, featuring a wide array of *Voices on Leadership*.

DEFINING LEADERSHIP

A leader can be defined as someone who leads people, a project, or a mission from one phase to another—not strictly for their own purpose but for the (perceived) benefit of others. Of course, that's just one of many definitions, and in this book, we focus on leadership of other people.

Since there are so many aspects of leadership, it has been defined by numerous people over the centuries. After all, there have been leaders of armies, ball clubs, space exploration, politics, protests, unions, and, of course, businesses. With leadership playing such a significant role in our world, it's no wonder so many people have had something to say (or write) about it. In fact, the late Ralph Stogdill, Professor Emeritus at Ohio State University and known for his research and publications on leadership and organizations, said, "There are almost as many definitions of leadership as there are persons who have attempted to define the concept."

Here are some pertinent quotes that define just ten of the many facets of strong leadership:

1. *On leading from within*: "Successful leadership is leading with the heart, not just the head. [Such leaders] possess qualities like empathy, compassion and courage." —Bill George: Former CEO of Medtronics and Ethics Professor at Harvard Business School

2. *On facing challenges*: "The ultimate measure of a man is not where he stands in moments of comfort and convenience, but where he stands at times of challenge and controversy." —Martin Luther King Jr.

3. *On gaining knowledge*: "Leadership and learning are indispensable to each other." —John F. Kennedy

4. *On getting the most from others*: "The task of leadership is not to put greatness into people, but to elicit it, for

the greatness is there already." —John Buchan, Novelist, Historian and former Governor General of Canada

5. *On inspiring others*: "If your actions inspire others to dream more, learn more, do more and become more, you are a leader." —John Quincy Adams

6. *On serving others*: "People don't care how much you know until they know how much you care. —John C. Maxwell, leadership expert and founder of EQUI, and international leadership development organization

7. *On keeping a low profile*: "A leader is best when people barely know he exists, when his work is done, his aim fulfilled, they will say: We did it ourselves." —Lao Tzu, Chinese philosopher and founder of Taosim

8. *On moving forward*: "The task of the leader is to get his people from where they are to where they have not been." —Henry Kissinger

9. *On achievement*: "Leadership is a process whereby an individual influences a group of individuals to achieve a common goal." —Peter Northouse, Professor of communications and author of several leadership books

10. *On understanding those you are leading*: "He who cannot be a good follower cannot be a good leader." —Aristotle

Of course, communication and patience are also cornerstones of leadership. And as you will read in this section, there are so many other ways to define a good leader. It should also be noted that there have always been, and still are, leaders who defy almost everything listed in the upcoming pages. They prey on weakness, fear, and even desperation in people, and preach "better days" ahead if you follow their lead, which is rigid, actually an agenda, and not in the best interest of those who choose to (or are forced to) follow. They can be powerful leaders, but they are not improving the well-being of their followers or employees. Some major companies have had such leaders and seen disastrous results. Unfortunately, as we've seen throughout history, such leaders, in business or elsewhere, often attain some of their goals before losing their leadership positions. The point is, while we celebrate the positive potential of leadership in the upcoming pages, it's worth noting that not all leaders are leading people in a positive direction. Fortunately, most are trying to.

CHAPTER

1

22 QUALITIES THAT MAKE A GREAT LEADER

Adam and Jordan Bornstein

Not all leaders are alike; in fact, they run the gamut from authoritative to leading by consensus. While they share the same title, they don't share the same leadership abilities or qualities, many of which are not necessarily "in the manual," so to speak.

Much of leadership stems from the personality traits, plus the innate and learned behaviors that make up the individual. Generally speaking, these intangibles are hard to measure, such as confidence, passion, integrity, open-mindedness, and various other qualities that come from within each of us. These qualities put you in touch with yourself and, more significantly, with the people you will be leading. They allow you to have an impact on your followers. After all, if a leader has no impact on those being led, then, no matter how much leadership training they have had, they will not make a great leader.

Below are 22 qualities that make great leaders, gathered from various sources, including CEOs, authors, founders, a former governor, and others. Consider which qualities you possess and those you need to further develop.

1. *Focus*. "It's been said that leadership is making important but unpopular decisions. That's certainly a partial truth, but I think it underscores the importance of focus. To be a good leader, you cannot major in minor things, and you must be less distracted than your competition. To get the few critical things done, you must develop incredible selective ignorance. Otherwise, the trivial will drown you." —Tim Ferriss, bestselling author, host of The Tim Ferriss Show, https://tim.blog

2. *Confidence.* "A leader instills confidence and 'followership' by having a clear vision, showing empathy and being a strong coach. As a female leader, to be recognized I feel I have to show up with swagger and assertiveness, yet always try to maintain my Southern upbringing, which underscores kindness and generosity. The two work well together in gaining respect." —Barri Friedman Rafferty, partner and president, Ketchum Inc.

3. *Transparency.* "I've never bought into the concept of 'wearing the mask.' As a leader, the only way I know how to engender trust and buy-in from my team and with my colleagues is to be 100 percent authentically me—open, sometimes flawed, but always passionate about our work. It has allowed me the freedom to be fully present and consistent. They know what they're getting at all times. No surprises." —Keri Potts, senior director of communications, ESPN

4. *Integrity.* "Our employees are direct reflections of the values we embody as leaders. If we're playing from a reactive and obsolete playbook of needing to be right instead of doing what's right, then we limit the full potential of our business and lose

quality talent. If you focus on becoming authentic in all your interactions, that will rub off on your business and your culture, and the rest takes care of itself." —Gunnar Lovelace, co-CEO and cofounder, Thrive Market

5. *Inspiration*. "People always say I'm a self-made man. But there is no such thing. Leaders aren't self-made; they are driven. I arrived in America with no money or any belongings besides my gym bag, but I can't say I came with nothing. Others gave me great inspiration and fantastic advice, and I was fueled by my beliefs and an internal drive and passion. That's why I'm always willing to offer motivation—to friends or strangers on Reddit. I know the power of inspiration, and if someone can stand on my shoulders to achieve greatness, I'm more than willing to help them up." —Arnold Schwarzenegger, former governor of California

6. *Passion*. "You must love what you do. In order to be truly successful at something, you must obsess over it and let it consume you. No matter how successful your business might become, you are never satisfied and constantly push to do something bigger,

better, and greater. You lead by example, not because you feel like it's what you should do, but because it is your way of life." —Joe Perez, cofounder, Tastemade

7. *Innovation.* "In any system with finite resources and infinite expansion of population—like your business, or like all of humanity—innovation is essential for not only success but also survival. The innovators are our leaders. You cannot separate the two. Whether it is by thought, technology, or organization, innovation is our only hope to solve our challenges." —Aubrey Marcus, founder and CEO, Onnit

8. *Patience.* "Patience is really courage that's meant to test your commitment to your cause. The path to great things is always tough, but the best leaders understand when to abandon the cause and when to stay the course. If your vision is bold enough, there will be hundreds of reasons why it 'can't be done' and plenty of doubters. A lot of things have to come together—external markets, competition, financing, consumer demand, and always a little luck—to pull off something big." —Dan Brian, COO, TV Time

9. *Stoicism.* "It's inevitable: We're going to find ourselves in some real shit situations, whether they're costly mistakes, unexpected failures, or unscrupulous enemies. Stoicism is, at its core, accepting and anticipating this in advance so that you don't freak out, react emotionally, and aggravate things further. Train our minds, consider the worst-case scenarios, and regulate our unhelpful instinctual responses—that's how we make sure shit situations don't turn into fatal resolutions." —Ryan Holiday, author of *The Obstacle Is the Way*, and former director of marketing, American Apparel

10. *Wonkiness.* "Understanding the underlying numbers is the best thing I've done for my business. As we have a subscription-based service, the biggest impact on our bottom line was to decrease our churn rate. Being able to nudge that number from 6 percent to 4 percent meant a 50 percent increase in the average customer's lifetime value. We would not have known to focus on this metric without being able to accurately analyze our data." —Sol Orwell, director of strategy, Examine.com

11. *Authenticity.* "It's true that imitation is one of the greatest forms of flattery, but not

when it comes to leadership—and every great leader in my life, from Mike Tomlin to Olympic ski coach Scott Rawles, led from a place of authenticity. Learn from others, read autobiographies of your favorite leaders, pick up skills along the way . . . but never lose your authentic voice and opinions and, ultimately, how you make decisions." —Jeremy Bloom, former Olympic athlete, author of Fueled by Failure, and cofounder/CEO, Integrate

12. *Open-mindedness.* "One of the biggest myths is that good business leaders are great visionaries with dogged determination to stick to their goals no matter what. It's nonsense. The truth is leaders need to keep an open mind while being flexible and adjust if necessary. When in the startup phase of a company, planning is highly overrated and goals are not static. Your commitment should be to invest, develop, and maintain great relationships." —Daymond John, CEO, The Shark Group and FUBU; Shark on ABC's *Shark Tank*, bestselling author and speaker, daymondjohn.com

13. *Decisiveness.* "In high school and college, to pick up extra cash, I would often referee recreational basketball games. The mentor

who taught me how to officiate gave his refs one important piece of advice that translates well into the professional world: 'Make the call fast, make the call loud, and don't look back.' In marginal situations, a decisively made wrong call will often lead to better long-term results and a stronger team than a wishy-washy decision that turns out to be right." —Scott Hoffman, owner, Folio Literary Management

14. *Personableness*. "We all provide something unique to this world, and we can all smell when someone isn't being real. The more you focus on genuine connections with people and look for ways to help them— rather than just focus on what they can do for you—the more likable and personable you become. This isn't required to be a great leader, but it is to be a respected leader, which can make all the difference in your business." —Lewis Howes, former NFL player and New York Times bestselling author of The School of Greatness

15. *Empowerment*. "Many of my leadership philosophies were learned as an athlete. My most successful teams didn't always have

the most talent but did have teammates with the right combination of skills, strengths, and a common trust in each other. To build an overachieving team, you need to delegate responsibility and authority. Giving away responsibilities isn't always easy. It can be harder to do than completing the task yourself, but with the right project selection and support, delegating can pay off in dividends. It is how you truly find people's capabilities and get the most out of them." – Shannon Pappas, senior vice president, Beachbody LIVE

16. *Positivity*. "In order to achieve greatness, you must create a culture of optimism. There will be many ups and downs, but the prevalence of positivity will keep the company going. But be warned: this requires fearlessness. You have to truly believe in making the impossible possible." —Jason Harris, president and CEO, Mekanism

17. *Generosity*. "My main goal has always been to offer the best of myself. We all grow—as a collective whole—when I'm able to build up others and help them grow as individuals." —Christopher Perilli, creative director of Pixel Mobb, founder of Dojo Muscle

18. *Persistence.* "A great leader once told me, 'persistence beats resistance.' And after working at Facebook, Intel, and Microsoft and starting my own company, I've learned two major lessons: all great things take time, and you must persist no matter what. That's what it takes to be a leader: willingness to go beyond where others will stop." —Noah Kagan, Chief Sumo, AppSumo

19. *Insightfulness.* "It takes insight every day to be able to separate that which is really important from all the incoming fire. It's like wisdom—it can be improved with time, if you're paying attention, but it has to exist in your character. It's inherent. When your insight is right, you look like a genius. And when your insight is wrong, you look like an idiot." —Raj Bhakta, founder, WhistlePig Whiskey

20. *Communication.* "If people aren't aware of your expectations and they fall short, it's really your fault for not expressing it to them. The people I work with are in constant communication, probably to a fault. But communication is a balancing act. You might have a specific want or need,

but it's super important to treat work as a collaboration. We always want people to tell us their thoughts and ideas—that's why we have all these very talented people working with us." —Kim Kurlanchik Russen, managing partner, TAO Group

21. *Accountability.* "It's a lot easier to assign blame than to hold yourself accountable. But if you want to know how to do it right, learn from financial expert Larry Robbins. He wrote a genuinely humble letter to his investors about his bad judgment that caused their investments to falter. He then opened a new fund without management and performance fees—unheard of in the hedge fund world. This is character. This is accountability. It's not only taking responsibility; it's taking the next step to make it right." —Sandra Carreon-John, managing director, M&C Saatchi, greater New York City area

22. *Restlessness.* "It takes real leadership to find the strengths within each person on your team and then be willing to look outside to plug the gaps. It's best to believe that your team alone does not have all the answers—because if you believe that, it

> usually means you're not asking all the right questions." —Nick Woolery, VP of brand marketing, Stance Socks

As you can see, leaders from diverse backgrounds share qualities and strengths that have led them to success. There is universality when it comes to leadership that is bound by the human element. It's about how to treat people, interact, inspire, and bring out the best in others . . . which will also bring out the best in you, as a leader, if you possess the right qualities.

2

SEVEN TRAITS OF EXCEPTIONAL LEADERS

Sherrie Campbell

Emotions are the universal language. Although what triggers our emotions differs, what we feel and how we express those feelings are typically is typically very similar. Therefore, if we can feel our own pain, then we know what it is like when someone else feels pain. Because of this projective identification, it allows us to empathize and lead others with greater awareness and increased bonding. To be an exceptional leader, we must be able to place ourselves in the shoes of another and feel what they are feeling.

1. *Self-awareness*. Great leaders are deeply knowledgeable about themselves and committed to their own personal development. To be great, we must do the same. The most influential people on earth, those who have left the most significant impact, led from the heart. Empathy is not something we learn from a book. It is gained through suffering. From our suffering, we come to accept pain and challenge as integral parts of life and necessary for great leadership. Think about it: would you want to follow a leader who had never suffered? How would this person know what to do or how to lead us on the front lines if they've never been there before? To be great, we must know how to lead ourselves through our own fears in order to know how to lead others through theirs.

2. *Self-control*. Empathy is most easily sacrificed when we're upset, angry, or disappointed with another person. We tend to be the most hurtful and impatient in these situations. The important thing to try and practice is taking a moment to get clear before speaking.

Great leaders tell others when a conversation will need to wait until they are clear enough to communicate responsibly. There is wisdom to knowing that conversations can be placed on hold. We cannot be reactive and empathic in tandem. In taking some time, we are able to take in the feeling, experience, and perception of the other in a way that makes sense, or at least in a way that arouses questions can be asked with empathy rather than accusation. We get a lot further in business when we have enough empathy for the other to make sure and harness our own self-control before we speak.

3. *Communication*. Empathy is the great healer of miscommunication. It is the emotion that moves people and situations through times of being stuck. Without empathy, solutions are forceful rather than powerful. Exceptional leaders count on empathy as a catalyst for change. It makes communication a two-way, collaborative, reflective process. It allows for vulnerability. With empathy, people feel seen and important. To develop a working environment conducive to success, we must be able to meet people where they are. We must be able to understand, respect, and implement another person's point of view, rather than

only our own. This type of communication introduces the concept of fairness into the success equation.

4. *Other-centered*. When we're empathic, we care about how other people are. Exceptional leaders ask others how they are doing, what they need, and what they feel. This increases bonding, honesty, and connection. When we have a clear idea of how others feel about what they're doing, we can better support and guide them. When others trust that we support them, they realize they're not alone and without help. We must keep in mind that if we want others to be invested in what we're doing and to respond with cooperation to what we're asking, then we must consider their ideas and how they perceive who we are. To be great, we must use empathy to guide all aspects of our lives, allowing it to influence not only what we say, allowing it not only to influence what we say but also to influence how we say what we say and to direct the kinds of questions we need to ask. When these steps are taken, it naturally inspires the development of empathy within others.

5. *Boundaries*. Exceptional leaders expect to face situations where they realize the only way a

person on their team can grow is to either withdraw their support from that person or to set boundaries around their support in an effort to protect their generous nature. To remain empathic, great leaders know they must protect their hearts and put themselves first in negative situations. Through trial and error, we must also understand that there are people who can stay in our hearts but not in our lives or businesses. If we are dealing with a person incapable of empathy, we must separate from them. All it takes is one toxic person to short-circuit an entire team's path to success. It is impossible to work with someone who is constantly defensive and unwilling to listen or take feedback.

6. *Kindness.* Great leaders lead from the heart. They live the wisdom that is the kindness of their spirit; how they treat, think about, and relate to others makes all the difference when it comes to developing a cohesive team driven to succeed. When we're kind, we naturally come from a genuine and sensitive place. Exceptional leaders are kind and use empathy to guide their every word, deed, and action. When we have this, we are able to be kind— even to those we do not care for. This is not a weakness or vulnerability. To be empathic

is our greatest influence over others. There is truly no human quality that will take us further in life than kindness. We must not strive just to be successful. We must strive to be exceptional—anyone can be successful.

7. *Selfless*. Great leaders give back. They understand that they get more from giving than from getting. When we give back, it increases our own quality of life and our perception of what we have, and it reminds us to be thankful for our lives as we witness the impact we have on the lives of others. When we give back, we feel good. It reminds us of the love and abundance we have in our lives, inspiring us to continue to strive to succeed to have more and more to give back. To be exceptional, we must embrace the power that comes from giving. Giving back is relationship building. It is through an involvement in our communities that we develop quality relationships, which also give back to us. People want to be linked with others who are giving. People want to work for people and companies that care. Great leaders do not want to be remembered for their net worth; they would rather be remembered for how they made other people feel.

Exceptional leaders live by the Golden Rule. To be exceptional in our own right, we must do the same. We must put ourselves in the situation of others, ask how we would like to be treated in their situation, and do our best to provide them what they deserve. The more empathy we bring to our more challenging relationship problems, business negotiations, or disciplinary situations, the more successful we will be. Empathy, humility, kindness, and understanding all come from love. There is nothing more appealing to others than to be in the presence of a loving person. Exceptional leaders live this wisdom.

ARE YOU A LEADER OR A FOLLOWER?

Elinor Stutz

A recently televised interview with Mark Cuban was a delight to watch—in particular, Cuban's facial expressions, which said it all!

There was a tremendous disconnect between Cuban and the host regarding their varying viewpoints when it came to doing business and accepting change. The host took an old-school approach and was unwilling to embrace new ideas. Even worse, he wore a puzzled expression throughout the conversation as Cuban continued to speak about the new ways in which we conduct business today. Frustration apparently took hold of Cuban as he momentarily covered his face with his hands. Undoubtedly, he was trying to answer the host's remark with diplomacy.

The Problem

As creative businesspeople and employees express new ideas, it can leave some people bewildered and others frightened. The scare comes from the need to re-educate while still showing dedication to current work. Most people do not want to face change or the realization that they might be falling behind the curve. They certainly do not want to muster up the courage, along with the time, to learn something new. The statement, "We've always done it that way," remains the popular refrain from those who believe firmly in the status quo, whether or not it means lagging behind.

For those fearing change, new ideas are often seen as threats down to the core. It is for this very reason that remarks, such as, "Your idea is crazy and will never take off," are heard. Wilbur and Orville Wright often heard that comment— literally—as they tried to get their early attempts at the airplane to work. Yet such comments made them more determined than ever to show that their innovative idea would "take off."

Therefore, if you are the creative sort who hears offensive remarks about your latest idea, just smile. The nastier the critique, the greater your potential impact may be with your new approach. Reactions to your ideas are often the best indicators of whether you are among leaders or followers. It may take years for others to recognize the merits of your creativity, but if you remain steadfast and maintain a positive approach, you may be at the forefront of something great.

Excitement = Personal Success

Behaviors are great indicators of whether a new idea is worthwhile or if it is a waste of time. You can even tell how much you really believe in your new idea simply by your own behaviors. For example, as an innovator:

- You review the workday ahead as you awake.
- You are excited each morning to get started.
- Your focus is on the outcome.

The excitement increases your motivation to succeed. If you find that you are only marginally enthusiastic, then your own behavior is telling you that perhaps you should rethink your idea. However, if you are excited about an idea and decide to move ahead, you always need to remember that nothing is 100 percent, nor does everything work well 100 percent of the time. So, on those occasions when an exciting project does not work out as you anticipated, take the time to learn from the experience and return to the drawing board with a new approach or a different project.

As an employee, are you keeping up with your daily duties, plus educating yourself on changes in your industry? And if you are an entrepreneur, are you keeping up to date with approaches to social media and all else that needs to be learned? Stay abreast of what your peers are working on and what they view as important. It helps to compare notes and provide insights for one another. And keep an open mind when it comes to new ideas and change. Hint: change is going to happen whether you want it to or not, so you may need to heed the words of Mark Cuban or anyone else talking about the changing business landscape. These people are leaders. As you experience success with the new strategies, share what you learn with others so they can also succeed. Not only will you help many in the process, but your following will grow with a well-established personal brand in place. Your career will advance as you become known as an innovative leader in your field. The best reward is when people take the time to thank you.

ENTREPRENEUR VOICES SPOTLIGHT: INTERVIEW WITH MATT MAYBERRY

In his senior year of high school football, Matt Mayberry played on both sides as a middle linebacker on defense and a fullback on offense. He scored 36 touchdowns in 12 games . . . yes, 36! For his efforts, he received 19 scholarship offers, from which, he decided to become a Hoosier at Indiana University. After four stellar years as a middle linebacker, he landed in the NFL on the Chicago Bears. Then, in a pre-season game, Mayberry suffered an ankle injury, which at the age of 23, changed his life.

We caught up with Mayberry to ask him a few questions about his journey toward a life of leadership and what advice he might give to aspiring leaders.

Entrepreneur: What motivated you to follow a new path?

Mayberry: When I learned I was seriously injured and was going to be out for about nine months, I was miserable and depressed. It was during that time of sulking around that

I was asked to speak at an event. My first reaction was to decline. I wasn't very good at public speaking; in fact, I got a D in it in college. But for whatever reason, after I hung up the phone and thought about my current situation, I decided to pick up and call the event planner back. I told him I wanted to do the event. It was that event that began my new passion—when I got done with that speaking engagement, I knew speaking was what I was put here to do for the rest of my life.

Entrepreneur: In your speaking engagements, you talk about the importance of becoming a transformational leader. How do you define a "transformational leader"?

Mayberry: Transformational leaders want to develop more leaders, and they do that by developing the leadership and growth of the people they are leading. It all starts with something as simple as caring more about their people. There are a lot of leaders who let their leadership position become more of an ego thing, but a transformational leader wants to see people move from one place to another—to a better place. It's not about the leader but about the people being led.

Entrepreneur: Are there ways to become a transformational leader?

Mayberry: First, you need to start caring more. Companies like Google or Infusionsoft make the point of stating "we listen, we care, we serve," are dominating their space, and do so by helping their employees achieve their personal goals. Infusionsoft even has someone holding the position of dream manager. This is someone who goes over personal goals with each employee. This could be anything from wanting a vacation in Hawaii with their families to running a marathon. The dream manager helps their employees move forward to achieve these personal goals. The results have been astounding.

It's also important to be obsessed with culture. The best leaders are obsessed with the culture of the organization and know how important it is to have the right people on board, people who buy into the company culture. The New England Patriots franchise is the "Apple" of the sports world, from owner Robert Kraft to head coach Bill Belichick—dominating their market because they are obsessed about culture. You can't move that needle forward in business or get to that vision of winning Super Bowls unless you demand a certain type of culture when everyone comes to work. A lot of people say they are concerned about culture, but are they hiring and firing based on that culture? 'Everything rises and falls with leadership,' as John C. Maxwell says, and that includes the culture of an organization.

Entrepreneur: Is there anything else that distinguishes transformational leaders?

Mayberry: All transformational leaders have positive attitudes. Positive leaders keep a positive vision—even when negativity hits. Positivity won't guarantee that you will win, but negativity will guarantee that you will lose. A trait of all transformational leaders is to keep that positive vision—even when negativity and failure strike.

NINE WAYS TO RECOGNIZE A REAL LEADER

Nicolas Cole

Leadership is a trait many are quick to claim but few truly deserve.

To be a leader does not mean wearing the title of "leader." It's not something you choose to be one minute and then choose not to be the next. A leader is not a leader simply because they have been promoted. And a leader is not someone who sits in a position of management.

None of those things are what truly make a real leader. Here are the things that do:

1. *A real leader listens first and acts second.* Someone who jumps to conclusions without first seeking to understand what has taken place has made a fatal error—for themselves and their team. In order to lead people effectively, you have to take the time to listen and see things from someone else's perspective. This goes to the idea of being other-centered. What is this person saying? What is their point? Where are they coming from? You have to put yourself in their shoes to fully understand the situation.

2. *A real leader doesn't make decisions in the heat of the moment.* You know those bosses who get all riled up and then start rapidly firing people? That's not a leader. That's a trigger-happy manager on a power trip—and there's a difference. A leader waits until the heat of the moment has passed so they can give solid thought to the situation before coming to a conclusion. Real leaders know how to take a deep breath and remain calm before evaluating and responding to a situation.

3. *A real leader knows what they don't know.* It's dangerous when someone claims to "know

everything." A good leader is OK with not having all the answers and knowing that they will find the people who do. They don't see it as a weakness—because it's not. It's actually a strength—it shows strong self-awareness and the ability to seek out, and take advice from, experts in areas in which they do not have the same level of knowledge or expertise.

4. *A real leader never wants to be the smartest person in the room.* If someone surrounds themselves with people less qualified than they are simply to remain in a position of power, then they obviously feel threatened. You never want to be the smartest person in the room—and if you are, you're in the wrong room. Great leaders know this and seek to surround themselves with masters of their crafts. The leaders job is to "conduct the orchestra."

5. *A real leader celebrates the process as much as the rewards.* True leaders know that greatness is not something that happens immediately. Greatness is the result of hours, days, and weeks of diligent practice and effort. They celebrate the process and the day-to-day hustle as much as they do the big grand finale.

6. *A real leader gives constructive, not negative, feedback.* There is a difference between "constructive criticism" and plain negativity. People who spew negativity aren't doing anything to help anyone. A great leader looks for ways in which they can help—not ways they can tear others down in the process. Such a leader wants to see someone else succeed from such positive feedback. To do this effectively, a real leader needs to be someone who does not feel threatened when other people shine.

7. *A real leader does what has to be done.* Anyone who says "that's not my job" isn't leading by example. People need to stay in their lanes and be responsible for their own work, but when there's a fire and it's all hands on deck, a leader doesn't step back and say, "All right, everyone, go figure it out." They get right to work along with everyone else.

8. *A real leader cultivates a positive culture.* Being results-driven is great, but a culture that produces results has to be healthy in some way, shape, or form. And creating that culture takes hard work. A great leader knows they are not the center of attention—what's more important is creating an environment where

others feel empowered to succeed, bring ideas to the table, and think for themselves.

9. *A real leader always finds a way.* Anyone who says, "It's impossible; we can't," isn't fit to lead. A true leader knows there is always a way. It might not be the way anyone had originally planned for, but it's a way nonetheless. Great leaders find the roads less traveled and do whatever needs to be done in order to get the collective over the obstacle(s) ahead.

FIVE KEYS TO INSPIRING LEADERSHIP, NO MATTER YOUR STYLE

Gwen Moran

Forget the stereotypical leadership image of a buttoned-up person in a gray suit hauling around a hefty briefcase. Today, standout leaders come in all shapes and sizes. They could be a blue jeans-clad marketing student running a major ecommerce company out of their dorm room. Or they might be the next salt-and-pepper-haired, barefoot Steve Jobs, presenting a groundbreaking new device at a major industry conference.

"Our research indicates that what really matters is that leaders are able to create enthusiasm, empower their people, instill confidence, and be inspiring to the people around them," says Peter Handal, chairman and CEO of New York City-based Dale Carnegie Training, a leadership-training company.

That's a tall order. However, as different as leaders are today, there are some things great leaders do every day. Here, Handal shares his five keys for effective leadership.

1. *Face challenges*. Great leaders are brave enough to face challenging situations and deal with them honestly. Whether it's steering through a business downturn or getting struggling employees back on track, effective leaders meet these challenges openly. Regular communication with your staff, informing them of both good news and how the company is reacting to challenges will go a long way toward making employees feel like you trust them and that they're unlikely to be hit with unpleasant surprises.

   "The gossip at the coffee machine is usually ten times worse than reality," says Handal. "Employees need to see their leaders out there—confronting that reality head-on."

2. *Win trust.* "Employees are more loyal and enthusiastic when they work in an environment run by people they trust. Building that trust can be done in many ways. The first is to show employees that you care about them," explains Handal, suggesting that you take an interest in your employees beyond the workplace. Don't pry, he advises, but ask about an employee's child's baseball game or college graduation. Let your employees know that you're interested in their success, and discuss their career paths with them regularly.

"When employees, vendors, or others make mistakes, don't reprimand or correct them in anger. Instead, calmly explain the situation and why their behavior or actions weren't correct, as well as what you expect in the future. When people know that you aren't going to berate them and that you have their best interests at heart, they're going to trust you," says Handal.

3. *Be authentic.* "If you're not a suit, don't try to be one. Employees and others dealing with your company will be able to tell if you're pretending to be someone you're not," explains Handal. That could make them question what else about you might be inauthentic. Have

a passion for funky shoes? Wear them. Are you an enthusiastic and hilarious presenter? Get them laughing. "Use your strengths and personality traits to develop your personal leadership style."

4. *Earn respect.* When you conduct yourself in an ethical way and model the traits you want to see in others, you earn the respect of those around you. Leaders who are perceived as not "walking their talk" typically don't get very far, notes Handal. This contributes to employees and other stakeholders having pride in the company, which is an essential part of engagement, adds Handal. Also, customers are less likely to do business with a company if they don't respect its values or leadership.

5. *Stay curious.* "Good leaders remain intellectually curious and committed to learning. They're inquisitive and always looking for new ideas, insights, and information," Handal says, "The best leaders understand that innovation and new approaches can come from many places and are always on the lookout for knowledge or people who might inform them and give them an advantage."

"The most successful leaders I know are truly very curious people. They're interested in the things around them, and that contributes to their vision," says Handal.

It's worth noting that Handal's recommendations do not require training or even years of experience. Each of the keys mentioned comes from within the individual leader. To be the best leader you can be and bring out the best in others stems soley from an internal desire to have the resolve to face challenges or to be authentic, or the desire to stay curious and keep learning.

6

FIVE ATTRIBUTES OF THE SUPER SUCCESSFUL

Tor Constantino

During my 25-plus years as a journalist, corporate communications executive, and entrepreneur, I've had the opportunity to directly work and interact with some of the most successful people in the world.

Whether it was a billionaire business leader, a hall-of-fame athlete, or former U.S. president—there are five attributes all of them share.

1. Capable Advisors

One of the greatest lessons in life is that teams make better decisions than individuals. Every successful person I have ever worked with has a team of capable advisors who provide expertise, counsel, wisdom, insight, and ideas to help make the best decisions possible.

Perhaps most important, these advisors are willing to tell the "alpha" when and why the leader is misguided or mistaken. That resistance to group-think plays a critical role in the continuing advance of the individual pacesetters.

When selecting advisors, it is also important that a leader carefully scrutinizes all candidates. You want to avoid people who are yes men or women or have their own agendas. Advisors need an understanding of the business and the goals of the company and the leader. After all, advisors who cannot provide advice that meets your level of knowledge are unlikely to be helpful.

2. Incredible Stamina

Each of these leaders also has an otherworldly level of stamina—physically, mentally, and emotionally. I've been continually amazed at their ability to keep moving forward and accomplish what other people are unwilling or unable to do by sheer velocity of action.

While they intentionally take time to rest and recharge, it seems like they prefer to briefly take their foot off the gas when they're metaphorically coasting downhill so as not to lose any momentum. It's akin to how large Army personnel carriers refuel in flight—coasting through the sky while taking on new energy instead of stopping to recharge.

I can't explain how they continue to sustain that level of stamina for years on end other than to assume that it's some high-octane blend of nature and nurture.

Regardless, they have one gear, and it's "GO."

3. Intellectually Curious

While there are always exceptions to the rule, the most successful individuals are inquisitive, life-long learners. They demonstrate an intrinsic drive to understand things—circumstances and people.

Interestingly, sometimes their curiosity doesn't even directly benefit their immediate project, initiative, or business. It's almost like they have a huge, internal neon sign that only they can see that alternately flashes between "what if?" and "why not?"

Thanks to technology, leaders are now able to dig deeper into areas in which they are curious and easily store much of the material they find. Leaders often use their rare quiet moments, or down time, to further explore what they have found.

4. Gracious

All of us have seen or known successful people who were flat-out jerks. In most instances, those individuals are not successful because of their rude behavior (unless that's their intentional shtick), but rather in spite of it.

The reality is that partners, associates, vendors, investors, and customers prefer to engage with individuals who are gracious and easy to get along with.

Simply stated, manners matter—even (or perhaps especially) when you reach the top of your field.

5. Positive Outlook

Lastly, the most successful people I know have a bubbling optimism that the future will be better and brighter than today. I believe their forward-focused exuberance is driven in large part by their internal locus of control that makes them believe that they have the power, ability, talent, and resources to positively impact and shape that future.

Even if they can't change the world, they are absolutely convinced that they can change their respective part of it.

While there's a seemingly unending list of attributes that successful people have, these five traits were universally shared by the dozen uber-successes with whom I've personally engaged.

If these attributes are not direct causes of success, they are most certainly correlated with it.

PART I
DEFINING LEADERSHIP—
REFLECTIONS

As you can see by the preceding chapters, leadership is largely defined by the qualities, traits, and attributes of the individual. Being gracious, staying curious, having patience, earning respect while holding people accountable, and being able to face challenges, while remaining calm, are among the many qualifications that factor into success as a leader.

There is no one-size-fits-all definition of a leader. Most often, a successful leader is defined by successful results, which, of course, vary entirely on the desired outcomes. Success often makes others retrace the steps of the leader; Steve Jobs was quoted as saying, "Innovation distinguishes between a leader and a follower." Of course, there are exceptions, where leaders stumbled their way along and just happened to fall upon success, and conversely, there are great leaders who never quite have the opportunity to achieve their ultimate goals. In most cases, however, you will find that leaders whose personal characteristics influence people to follow their lead, and who empower people and bring out their strengths, are most often defined as great leaders.

DEVELOPING LEADERSHIP

There are two types of leadership: intentional and improvisational. In the world of public speaking, from stand-up comics to politicians, there are many people who think they can "wing-it" with great success. Yet, there are few who really can. The best public speakers are well-prepared, even if they make it sound extemporaneous, and the best leaders fall into that same category. By being prepared, they are being intentional leaders.

If you are leading by intention, there is an aspect of planning that precipitates your introduction to the role. It is this preparation that guides you once you have assumed a leadership position. You are not only learning through training, reading about leadership, and honing your skills, but you are actively tapping into those qualities, traits, and attributes we discussed in Part I. Someone who is an intentional leader has goals, plans, milestones, and an approach to reaching their desired outcomes. Intentional leaders don't merely have a meeting agenda but have a preconceived idea of how they can best use the meeting in a productive manner. Which teams will report first and why? Which issues will demand more attention? Who will be called on to speak? They will know when to actively seek out participation. They will intentionally try to get everyone involved in a comfortable manner. They may, in fact, not even invite people or teams to the meeting that need not be there.

Leading by intent is working with a plan and even having a plan in place to expect the unexpected. Intentional leaders will know that a change in the daily operations, technology, or even scheduling may be difficult for some employees (since change is always anxiety-provoking for some people). This leader will intentionally set aside time to talk with those individuals who have difficulty with such adjustments. They will be prepared when someone needs to come in and let off steam. As a leader, they will foresee such situations and not react impulsively. Returning to the earlier comic analogy, it is akin to the comic who is prepared to respond to a heckler during their act. "Hey, I don't come to your place of work and yell at you, do I?" responds the comic, as if it's an off-the-cuff answer. Preparation, training, and anticipating what comes next are among the skills that highlight intentional leadership.

The contrast is the leader who has worked their way up the ladder, then gets promoted to a leadership role without having leadership skills or training. They do not understand how much responsibility is associated with their new leadership position. As a result, they use the "fly-by-the-seat-of-your-pants" improvisational approach, which rarely works.

Many leaders find themselves having to double back and take a trip around the leadership learning curve. Others see potential opportunities and develop their leadership skills in advance. Either way, leadership is a developed skill. Some people do have the innate abilities to lead people. Some know how to command attention or are simply charismatic or charming. Others are extroverts by nature. These may be beneficial skills to have, but the fine points of good leadership need to be learned and the skills need to be developed. This section focuses on developing those traits and skills that create strong, intentional leaders.

The following chapters not only dissect the skills you need to develop within yourself to be a great leader but will also equip you with strategies to develop leaders within your business or team. As an intentional leader, it is as necessary to prepare yourself for the challenges ahead as it is to prepare others to become leaders themselves.

FOUR THINGS THE NEW LEADER OF AN ORGANIZATION SHOULD DO RIGHT AWAY

Tom Gimbel Mesh

Changing leadership is an adjustment process for all concerned. How well the new leader and the current employees will interact is a source of concern on everyone's part, as are the cultural ramifications within the organization. It's a period of excitement, growing pains, and hope. As the incoming leader in an existing organization, it's largely up to you to take the first steps in easing the transition.

While earning the trust and loyalty of an entire organization is a challenge, there are four things an incoming leader can do right away to hit the ground running and earn support:

1. Get to Know All Levels of Staff

In some situations, new leadership can mean staff changes across the board. But in most cases, tenured staffers remain in place. The new head coach of a sports team can be great, but he has to start with the players the team already has on their roster. Focus on earning the trust and respect of those retained staff members.

United Airlines CEO Oscar Munoz is a great example of a new leader who came in and got to know people at all levels. He noticed "there was a high level of distrust and disengagement with employees" when he came in. That's not unusual. When new leadership takes over, some people may be skeptics at first.

Munoz revamped company morale in a grassroots way. He spent time in the maintenance hangar with the mechanics, and he stood on the tarmac with the baggage handlers; he showed he genuinely cared about the people who were working toward achieving the company vision. Such authenticity gets people re-engaged. It helps break down barriers between ranks and shows that the leader is one of the people. And often, the best and most innovative ideas will be the ones that come from the people with their ears to the ground every day.

2. Inspire Camaraderie

Even though Marissa Mayer's time at Yahoo! has been panned, what she attempted to do made strategic sense. She came under fire when she ended remote work and mandated employees come into the office. The criticism made it seem like she was taking a personal stand against working remotely. She wasn't. It was about fixing a broken company culture. If the company had been succeeding when she took over, it would be a different story.

Mayer understood the importance of having people in close proximity to their bosses and colleagues. People need that fire in their seat that comes from the energy in a room full of people working together toward a common goal. It may mean having more people in the office more often, or in some cases, knocking down some of the partitions so that people are able to engage with one another. There are many ways to inspire camaraderie, which can be so important in a company's culture.

3. Hold People Accountable

Hold employees accountable. Encourage them to take ownership of their roles and speak up when they have opinions and ideas. Then, showcase the successes that come as a result.

I tell my staff all the time: if you speak up at work, you will have to do something to prove your thoughts and feelings are valid. It pushes you to act. Too often, people assume that someone else will figure it out. But often, they don't. Speaking up is not about complaining; it's about executing. Employees need to be part of the solution.

4. Identify the Superstars and Build on Them

Every leader has their own way of gauging top talent, but too often, it happens indirectly. For new leaders, there's a benefit to taking a staff inventory right away. Pay close attention and determine the key producers. It will take some time to get an accurate picture of people's abilities (the amount of time will depend on the size of the company), but putting in extra time to know the staff in the early phases will lay a foundation for identifying the key players the company needs to invest in and recruit again.

As you get a feel for the staff, make a three-column list. In one column, you have 3, 4, or maybe even 10 or 20 names, (depending on the size of the company) of people you believe are the best performers. In the second column, list the most competent today. And in the third column, list who you believe has the most potential to be great. Each list will have mostly different names, but there will be rare cases where there is some overlap. These lists might change as you make more observations over time. The point is to have a visual running reference for who needs more challenging work, extra attention, or corporate grandparenting. It's about making sure the company's future is in the best hands.

8

FOUR STRATEGIC STEPS TO BUILDING LEADERSHIP DEVELOPMENT PROGRAMS

William Hall

Your business is growing and hiring people at an amazing rate. Customers love your product, and it's gaining greater and greater attention. At the same time, you've noticed yourself growing ever more nervous about the byproducts of this success: increased competitive pressure and employee fragmentation. In fact, these two realities have you concerned: can you effectively sustain this level of success?

As we all know, success is like blood in shark-infested waters: it creates competition at an amazing rate. To fend off competition, many companies expand within the market faster than others, gaining a larger foothold and raising the barriers to entry. In many cases, this works. But such rapid growth creates an employee base with widely varying skills and focus. As a result, the company's strategic alignment looks like a spilled package of dried spaghetti. Employees are pointing in an infinite number of directions.

The good news is that with some thought, planning, and competent guidance, you can turn this challenge into a killer weapon. Imagine the power of a shared focus with all workers aligned behind the company's direction and execution plan. It's very possible. And it starts with effective leadership and corporate training. You can use four core steps to build a strategically critical leadership-development program within your growing company.

Step 1: Task Your HR Head to Build a Program Around Strategic Outcomes

To begin, you'll need to work with human resources to assemble a program that focuses on accelerating strategic execution. It all starts with effective leadership development. Move a step or two down the organization chart, and you'll quickly see managers who have a foggy idea of your company's strategy and what it will take to execute it.

Worse yet, moving a layer or two below that will reveal employees who don't know the corporate strategy at all. Those who are somewhat familiar with the overall concepts have little idea how they fit in or how they can help execute the strategy. Your leadership-development program should concentrate on aligning people with corporate strategic outcomes. Do this, and you'll immediately supercharge your strategic execution.

Step 2: Apply Training Content Directly to Business Methods, Products, and Results

Your company's training must be stepped up to a whole new level. Your new program should challenge the participants at a very deep level in leadership behavior, strategic fundamentals, and business acumen. Most significantly, the training will require hands-on learning.

It's likely you'll need to use tools such as business simulation, customized case studies with actual quantitative data, applied situational training, and more. Topics must be real, applicable, and challenging. Give your trainees a day in the life of the CEO.

Step 3: Demonstrate How the Training Will Prove Effective for Participants

Your lofty promise that "this will have a positive effect" can be difficult—and empty-sounding—for your employees to grasp. It's essential to engage training participants in exercises that demonstrate how these lessons will have financial or market impact.

For example, more effective budgets, personnel, and leadership might result in more productivity, lower employee attrition, and greater customer satisfaction. You can tailor a wide range of inexpensive tools to align with your training program and match leadership development with business outcomes.

Step 4: Determine the Feasibility of Integrating Executives in Leadership Training

Hands-on learning tools that apply training to actual strategic outcomes is complicated but well worth the effort. Involving executives in the training will go an exceptionally long way toward making this task easier.

Deep, usable learning takes place during open and applicable dialogues between executives and managers. It doesn't take long. Affording participants even 30 minutes with an executive after completing the hands-on training is invaluable.

This formula can be adapted to create hands-on learning for nearly any growing company. Make the content within the training highly relevant to the business and your employees' roles, and you'll align your entire organization behind your corporate strategy. It's the best way to speed up execution and ensure your company reaches its stated goals as soon as possible.

SIX MISTAKES ROOKIE LEADERS MAKE

Gordon Tredgold

The transition from technical expert to first-time leader is a difficult step and one that causes many to stumble and fail. I know this from personal experience.

In fact, I initially struggled to get the respect of my team and almost lost control and failed to deliver the project I was leading. Fortunately, I had a very supportive manager who stepped in and helped pull me through that ordeal so I could ultimately make the grade. But the lesson was clear: Too often, people are put in leadership positions without the appropriate training, and they struggle.

Here are six common mistakes that rookie managers make, which can cause them to fail.

1. *Believe they have all the answers.* When you appoint technical experts to leadership positions without the appropriate management skills, they believe that their technical experience will save them, and they start to believe that either they have, or need to have, all the answers. This can lead team members to feel uninvolved and uncommitted. New leaders need to understand that management, like any position, brings a new set of responsibilities. It may be a humbling feeling, especially for a top achiever, to take a step back and recognize that they will now need to seek out answers in their new role.

2. *Too hands-off.* What a lot of people fail to realize is that with every promotion comes more work—not less. When leaders make that mistake, they become hands-off, sitting in their offices and leaving everything to their team. As a leader, you are heavily involved in defining the goals, setting the vision, inspiring

the team, and leading the charge. Leadership is not a hands-off, paper-shuffling job; it's a hands-on job, especially when you are stepping into a new role. You need to get a feel for the job, which may mean getting your hands dirty to fully understand what the team does and what they need to accomplish the goals.

3. *Too hands on*. Just because you were the expert doesn't mean you need to be involved in everything. Your job is to lead the team— not necessarily to do the work for them. Sure, there may be times when you need to step in and get your hands dirty, but that should be the exception and not the rule. Once you familiarize yourself with the needs and responsibilities of your team, you will need to step back. This will allow your team to function with greater autonomy and come to you when there is a question or a problem.

4. *Micromanage every task*. Micromanagement is a productivity killer. No one wants their boss looking over their shoulder every two minutes asking, "Are we there yet?" It shows a lack of trust and that you don't respect their skills. It also creates great stress for the employees. You need to strike the right balance between giving

them enough space to do the job themselves and checking in to see how they are doing and if they need support.

5. *Create distance.* One of the worst and most common mistakes I see with new leaders and managers is when they create a distance between themselves and the people who work for them. They adopt the 'it's lonely at the top' mentality as a strategy for good leadership. Distance, however, often causes gaps in communication, which results in individuals, or teams, taking the wrong direction. When you create distance, you also make it difficult for people to feel engaged, and when teams become disengaged, results can suffer.

6. *Act like a friend instead of a manager.* It's good to be friendly, but you need to make sure that the friendship you have with your team doesn't impact your judgment or decision making. If you were previously one of the team, this can be a difficult balance to strike, as there is a good chance that you're already friends with many of them, especially if you have worked together for a while.

It doesn't mean you should immediately drop people as friends, but you need to be able to delineate between being a friend and being their boss. People will try and take advantage, but you need to be firm and do what's right and fair—and definitely don't play favorites. In the end, a good friend will respect you more for separating your friendship and your position as a manager.

It's not easy to make the transition from team member to team leader, but as you start on that journey, remember it's your job to engage, inspire, and support your team. They are the people who are going to do the bulk of the work, and your job is to put them in the position to be successful and then help them be successful.

THREE STRATEGIES FOR PROJECTING SUCCESS AND CONFIDENCE AS A LEADER

Rehan Ijaz

An old friend called me, and I enjoyed the opportunity to learn about where his life was taking him. During the discussion, he commented, "I can't believe the idiots I have to put up with at the office." It is easy to dismiss people around you, or beneath you on the corporate scale, as incompetent, but I've realized that everyone else's job always looks easier and less stressful than yours until you walk a mile in their shoes or sit for an hour in their cubicle.

Here are three keys to building that understanding and leading more effectively.

1. Develop the Heart of a Servant

As a leader, this is incredibly important to understand. Your job is to step into everyone's shoes and find ways to make their path less treacherous, stressful, and demoralizing. Keep in mind that a leader is in service to those around them, and the best ones do this so consistently that their team takes it for granted.

Serving your team's needs, without losing your status as their boss, is a balancing act. The key to taking the role of a servant is the projection of confidence. Well-established confidence in yourself is perfect for establishing the heart of a servant.

2. Physical Fitness and Presence Are Important

I've heard some of my colleagues lament the fact that "young and energetic" sometimes outweighs experience when opportunities to climb the corporate ladder present themselves.

The truth is, we're living in a youth-oriented culture, and since we cannot bottle that young and energetic feeling, the best thing every entrepreneur and corporate leader can do to (sort of) negate the advantages of youth is to stay fit! Thanks to the plethora of knowledge the human race has collected on health and wellness, it's possible to look fit and trim at any age. More than youth, physical fitness, and presence are valued by a company worried about the image of their team to the outside world. Don't let a date on a birth certificate define you. Fitness and vitality will help you exude confidence and project success.

3. Over-Prepare in Private

There are few things more frustrating than working for a leader who has little grasp of the facts or the reality surrounding an upcoming decision. A great leader takes the counsel of their team but has invested the time and energy to educate themselves on the situation as well. Counsel should be centered around providing a different perspective instead of a start-to-finish education on the problem.

Confident leaders serve their team best by being well-informed, current, and aggressively prepared. Spoiler alert: preparation is a key component to experiencing a favorable outcome. If you clearly understand what you want to achieve when you make your decision, and you have done the research to provide a foundation of facts, you can better nudge the conversation in a direction that leads to the outcome you are seeking.

The best salespeople, team leaders, and negotiators don't worry about who does the most talking. They worry more about the direction of the conversation. After all, if the conversation is headed in a direction that leads to your desired outcome, does it really matter who does the talking?

A confident leader understands the value of preparation and uses their depth of knowledge to steer the conversation. In the end, the participants feel ownership in the final decision, even if it was different from their original intention.

> *People are rewarded in public for what they practice for years in private.*
> —Tony Robbins

Great leaders commit to being amazing long before the meeting or moment their confident leadership is needed. They develop the habit of serving those around them, spending time in the gym to get in shape, and taking the necessary time in their offices to study in order to make the right decisions and develop the right strategies to support those decisions. The confidence that is projected in the moment is the result of hard work in private.

11

SIX COMPANY CHANGES TO DEVELOP MORE FEMALE LEADERS

Steffen Maier

Allegations of sexual harassment by the management of Uber, in early 2017,and initial apathy by human resources brought to the forefront the lack of progress we've made in gender equality. What former Uber employee Susan Fowler's story highlighted was that not only do women face direct discrimination from managers and peers, but when they speak out, they often feel the backlash in their opportunities for advancement.

The lack of female leaders in general, and especially in the tech world, is one of the most highly discussed challenges. All the industry giants have been criticized for continuing to have such low numbers of women on the board, in management positions, or even in the work force in general. This has caused many, such as Facebook, Google, and Apple to publicly release reports on their diversity statistics and commit to developing more female leaders. The numbers of women of color in leadership positions is even lower. A study by the AAUW in 2016 found that out of Standard and Poor's 500, only 4 percent of executives and managers were women of color.

Not only is this an issue about equality, but it also greatly impacts a company's bottom line. Studies show that companies that are more gender diverse are 15 percent more likely to outperform their competitors, and those that are more ethnically diverse are 35 percent more likely to outperform their competitors. Companies with more female leaders have also proved to be more profitable. In fact, studies have shown that women are typically rated as being more effective leaders overall than men by their reports, peers, and managers. So, why are there so few female leaders?

Unconscious Bias

While we may not realize it, everyone is subject to unconscious bias. The reason why it's so taboo is because people fear being labelled as sexist, racist, or prejudiced for acknowledging it. In fact, studies show that it's not just male managers who unconsciously stereotype women—female managers are also susceptible to unconscious bias against their female reports. Failing to acknowledge the potential for unconscious bias is your company's number-one mistake when it comes to developing female and minority leaders.

Even if your company has a clear policy against inequality in promotions and pay, why does it still happen? To find out, you have to look at the root causes.

Similarity Bias

Similarity bias is the tendency for people to want to help and mentor people who remind them of themselves when they were coming up in the company. As the majority of managers are still men, it's not uncommon for them to see themselves in a male report who may have the same personality and interests as them when they began working.

Even if unconscious, this can lead managers to favor certain reports with extra mentoring and, thereby, opportunities for development.

In Feedback

Feedback and performance reviews are essential to helping employees develop professionally and for companies to identify top performers for new positions. When unconscious bias finds its way into these important tools for advancement, it can cause women to be held back under the radar.

A joint 2016 study by McKinsey & Company and *Lean In* found that while both genders ask for feedback equally, women are 20 percent less likely to receive difficult feedback. The most common answer given is that managers don't want to seem "mean or hurtful."

Most managers already find it difficult to give constructive feedback even when their employees ask for it. If male managers hold on to an unconscious fear that women will be more likely to react emotionally to feedback, their female reports will not receive the same coaching opportunities as their male peers.

Adding another layer, a study by the Center for Talent Innovation found that two-thirds of men in senior positions pulled back from one-on-one contact with junior female employees for fear that they might be suspected of having an affair.

In Performance Reviews

What's more, when women receive feedback, studies show it is often vague and not tied to business outcomes. This means that, whether it's positive or constructive, women are less likely to be told what specific actions contributed to the team/company objectives or how they can improve. Meanwhile, their male colleagues are more likely to receive a clear picture of how they're doing and what they can do to improve.

People also have a tendency to see certain behaviors as primarily male or female. For example, assertiveness, independence, and authority are often stereotyped as "male," while supportive, collaborative, and helpful are perceived as typically "female." Therefore, studies show that when women demonstrate qualities typically associated with men, it is often criticized. For example, two studies in particular have shown that while men are often described as confident and assertive, for the same behavior, women are described as abrasive and off-putting.

There is no evidence, however, that men are more effective leaders. A 2012 study by Zenger and Folkman (http://zengerfolkman.com/media/articles/ZFCo.WP.WomenBetterThanMen.033012.pdf) sought to evaluate the effectiveness of male vs. female leaders in 16 leadership qualities. Overall, women were perceived as more effective and surpassed men in 12 categories—even those typically perceived as "male," such as taking initiative and driving for results.

Perhaps most convincing, a meta-analysis of 99 data sets from 95 studies conducted between 1962 to 2011, published in the *Journal of Applied Psychology*, similarly found that female leaders were rated by their reports, peers, and managers as being just as or even more effective than male leaders.

The interesting question is why do women continue to be overlooked for leadership positions? These studies may reveal some answers. For one, the meta-analysis showed that, while they're rated highly by others, many tend to underrate themselves in their self-assessments. Another, as mentioned previously, is the tendency to perceive the desired leadership skills as those regularly stereotyped as "male."

In today's flattening, collaborative, autonomous work atmosphere, companies are beginning to realize they want coaches—not managers. Some of the top qualities needed instead are emotional intelligence, coaching/mentoring, ability to motivate and engage through purpose, and empowering through autonomy and ownership. In effect, not only are our perceptions of female vs. male leaders incorrect, but our perceptions of what makes a great leader are also based on outdated stereotypes.

Here are six ways you can help your company develop more female leaders:

1. *Recognize the potential for unconscious bias.* Rather than making it a witch hunt, it's important to explain that the potential for bias is common, but there are ways that companies are helping their work forces to identify and combat it. Companies like Paradigm and Textio, for example, are helping major tech companies overcome this challenge by offering training sessions and workshops on implicit bias and opening their hiring practices to more diverse candidates. Meanwhile, Google has come up with its own internal program to help its people recognize unconscious bias. It has also publicly shared the slides and training materials it presents to its employees.

2. *If you think your feedback may be hurtful, you're giving it wrong.* If you're unconsciously worried about giving constructive feedback to a female report because you don't know how they'll take

it, you should consider how you're saying it. Anyone—whether a man or a woman—who receives strong criticism that isn't actionable will find it difficult to process. Remember these key practices: Never judge, always refer to specific examples of what was said or done, and provide suggestions for how the person can improve.

3. *Define top leadership qualities*. Without a common and agreed-upon set of top leadership qualities, it is more likely that people will hold onto the dominating stereotype of the typical "boss." Instead, take a page from Google's Project Oxygen. During this project, the company facilitated employee surveys, analyzed manager performance reviews, and interviewed the top managers within the company. As a result, they came up with eight key behaviors that the best managers possess.

Not surprisingly, not a single one conformed to the traditional authoritarian stereotype many still unconsciously think of. Instead, some of these included being a great coach, empowering the team and not micromanaging, and expressing interest/concern for team members' success and well-being.

Find out what qualities are most important for being a great leader in your company. Make sure this process is inclusive with feedback from employees, peers, and managers alike. The better you define what leadership looks like, the less likely future managers will be chosen based on outdated stereotypes.

4. *Integrate these qualities into your performance review process.* It's not enough to simply come up with a list of behaviors. The next step is to integrate them into your performance review process as core leadership competencies. Rather than asking if the person has leadership potential, ask people to review others based on their ability to coach, communicate effectively, or empower others. This will help both men and women develop the leadership skills needed to effectively manage your teams.

5. *Mentor reports.* Rather than making coaching an informal part of a manager's job, every manager should set up standing bimonthly one-on-one's and/or weekly strategic check-ins with each report. By making these one-on-one meetings standard for everyone, managers can ensure they're not unconsciously giving preference to certain employees over others.

6. *Tackle imposter syndrome.* Though often associated with women, studies show that imposter

syndrome (feeling you are not qualified when, in fact, you are) affects both sexes. It could very well be the reason why talented individuals aren't getting promoted within your organization. To address this common phenomenon, help train your employees to set challenging but attainable goals and teach them how to use these achievements to benchmark their progress—for themselves and their manager.

In a world that moves two steps forward and one step back, progress and equality for women, and especially those from minority backgrounds, has moved forward . . . slowly. Stories of sexual harassment emanating from Uber, Fox News, and various other companies simply mean that there is a long way to go to break long standing misconceptions and inappropriate behavior. Leaders need to find new approaches in business practices that take the gender bias out of the equation. It should be common sense, and good business sense, to treat everyone with dignity and respect and behave with appropriate decorum in a place of business, but like so many other cultural changes, progress is unfortunately slow moving.

12

FOUR WAYS A FOLLOWER CAN BECOME A LEADER

Anna Johansson

Do you consider yourself a follower? Have you always wanted to become a leader? What distinguishes the two?

Leadership comes with additional responsibility, but also additional opportunities, more respect, and more control over your life. While some people are content to avoid leadership, serving as cogs in bigger machines, the rest of us aspire to take charge of our own destinies. But if you're used to living your life and spending your career as a follower, is it even possible to become a leader?

Why Leadership Is Attainable

It's been said that leaders are born, not made, but there's evidence to the contrary. To determine why leaders can be made and aren't just naturally born, let's take a look at what it takes to be a successful leader:

- *Confidence*. Confidence comes naturally to some, but for everyone else, it's a "fake it 'til you make it" approach. Leaders only need to appear confident—it doesn't matter what they feel on the inside. As you grow as a leader, remember your successes, starting with the small ones. The more you realize the positives, the more confidence you will gain, so this is a skill that can be attained.

- *Knowledge*. There's no limit to how much knowledge a person can gain, so there's no attainability limit here.

- *Ability*. Abilities can be improved through practice. If you aren't inherently good in your niche, you can work to become better.

- *Decisiveness*. Decisiveness is another skill inherent to some but capable of being acquired by others. Making firm decisions and striving for resolve is something that can be practiced and improved. It often starts with gaining knowledge to make informed decisions and gaining confidence.

- *Respect*. You should demonstrate respect to everyone, regardless of whether you're a leader or a follower. If you truly can't demonstrate this quality, you don't have the right to be a leader. Also, remember that by being respectful of others you will also gain greater respect.

- *Commitment*. If you're interested in becoming a leader, you're already committed to your goals and ideals in some way. Making a commitment means being dedicated and staying the distance.

- *Communication*. Though some people make for naturally better communicators, you can sharpen your communicative abilities through practice. Remember, communication is not just about what you have to say, but also very much about how well you listen.

This isn't a comprehensive list, but these are fundamentals any leader should have. As you've noticed, all of them are directly obtainable, or at least imitable, making it possible for anyone to become a leader with the right motivation.

Attaining Leadership

We know leadership is attainable, so here are the four methods you can use to achieve it:

1. *Experience*. The first method simply comes with the territory. The more time you spend engaging in a specific industry, niche, or role, the better you'll get to know it. You'll learn the ins and outs of the trade, especially if you dabble in other areas, and eventually, you'll develop the knowledge, communicative abilities, and confidence it takes to be successful as a leader in this niche. This first path to leadership is a natural one, and it's all about gaining mastery over a specific area. Keep working hard and improving yourself, and eventually, you'll be the right fit for the job.

2. *Incremental growth*. You don't have to go from being a follower to a leader overnight—in fact, there are many professional positions that serve as intermediary roles between the two. Managers are a perfect example; they aren't making any drastic decisions or serving as visionaries for the organization,

but they are delegating, communicating, and organizing their own teams. Start seeking these intermediary "leadership" roles and inching your way up the ladder until you start feeling more comfortable in your leadership abilities. They will develop in time.

3. *Sheer will.* Of course, it's also possible to develop your abilities as a leader through sheer force of will, strange as it may sound. If you spend some time introspecting and evaluating what it takes to be a leader in your industry, you can make a list of all the abilities, skills, or points of knowledge you need to acquire and slowly work to acquire them. This method takes significant time, energy, and will, but it can lead you in the right direction for development.

4. *Necessity.* Sometimes, the best way to learn how to swim is to be thrown into the water. Since leadership abilities reliably develop with experience, in some cases, the best thing to do is to adopt a leadership role—such as starting your own business—regardless of how ready you are. You'll sink or swim by necessity, and the pressure of the situation will help you develop your necessary skills faster. It's a

scarier method to become a leader but a faster one.

These methods aren't the only ones you can use to spark your evolution into a leader, but they are some of the most reliable. Choose a path, drawing inspiration from others along the way if you hit obstacles or find yourself wanting something different from your journey. As long as you remain committed and aren't afraid of challenging or changing yourself, there's nothing that can stop you from becoming a great leader.

PART II
DEVELOPING LEADERSHIP— REFLECTIONS

Becoming a strong leader means being an intentional leader—one who takes the time and makes a concerted effort to learn, hone, acquire, copy, tap into these leadership skills, or even fake it until you make it. It means acquiring knowledge, gaining experience, and becoming other-centered. Remember, leadership is not strictly about the leader. That last sentence sounds obvious, but it is surprising how many leaders think it's all about them and not about the people they are leading. And while it is true that someone can be thrown into a leadership position and, like being thrown into a pool, learn to swim, it's less likely you will become a champion swimmer or a great leader without taking a lap around the leadership learning curve.

Companies should encourage leaders to grow and learn. This includes everything from offering seminars to podcasts to learning from their own experiences. Such training and having the availability to attain knowledge has influenced the methodology, style, and manners of dealing with the challenges that leaders possess today.

Of course, the best leaders recognize that leadership doesn't begin and end with them. Helping to create the next generation of leaders should be part of the plan. By answering the question "why?" frequently in regard to the work that is being done, you can explain not only the tasks, projects, and responsibilities associated with employment, but also the reasons behind them, providing the big picture of business operations to your team members. Also, allowing employees to see that you can be humble and that you don't know everything encourages them to look for solutions to problems. This helps them cultivate leadership abilities.

Ultimately, leadership comprises skills that you can continually develop, even once you are successful. It's not uncommon to hear successful leaders commenting on things that they learned after 20 or even 30 years into their tenure as leaders. It's also not unusual, after 20 or 30 years, to see leaders taking pride in younger leaders who have evolved their skills during their leadership.

LEADING FROM THE BOTTOM UP

There are two common types of management styles that leaders tend to adopt—top-down and bottom-up. Top-down management is an autocratic style, one which dominated business and industry for many years. In such a process, leaders typically make unilateral decisions. They set the goals and expectations, then review the progress of the organization. All changes in policies and processes come down from the leader. Top-down leadership can work effectively if the leader is well-versed in business, knowledgeable about the industry, well-organized, and has a realistic grasp on how to guide the company forward. In short, leaders in such companies must be very strong—in personality and in their ability to accomplish great things. They fair better when they also have the trust and respect of the people.

Conversely, such a leadership style suffers when the leader is not as well-versed as they should be or is unable to remain relevant and in step with the changes in the industry, economy, marketplace, and needs of the employees, as well as the wants (or needs) of the customers. Autocratic leaders, who are out of step with the times or refuse to change or do not listen to the guidance of others, can cause chaos.

Bottom-up management is a newer style of leadership and one that has come to the forefront in an age of smarter, savvier employees. It is especially popular in the ever-changing tech world. Leading from the bottom means involving everyone in the leadership process in some manner and taking into account their ideas, concerns, and feedback. It brings empowerment to employees at all levels; provides room for input and thorough meetings, messaging, and a host of communication tools; and unites everyone under the same goals (even in a large company). The "I make all the decisions" refrain of autocrats is replaced by a "we're in this together" mentality. In essence, instead of being "the boss," you're "the leader."

As a result of leading from the bottom up, there is a shared enthusiasm by teams as they are motivated to work harder. Team members are able to devise steps on their own to reach milestones and are empowered to make decisions when necessary. Everyone, from the bottom up, can use their talent more fully in this type of leadership environment, especially when they are treated with respect, acknowledged, praised for good work, and supported. The real advantage of the bottom-up leadership style is the basic idea that 10, 20, or 5,000 heads are better than one, especially when it comes to new concepts and innovative ideas.

Of course, there are drawbacks to the bottom-up leadership style. Getting input from many sources can be time-consuming and confusing, so leading from the bottom requires well-organized, open-minded leadership from someone who does not believe that they know everything and is even willing to take on the role of servant.

WHY LEADERS SHOULD VIEW THEMSELVES AS SERVANTS

Todd Wolfenbarger

Twenty years ago, I received a unique gift. This gift impacted my career by introducing me to a servant leadership model I've tried to emulate ever since.

I was living in Seattle and had taken off for Christmas Eve. It was a typical December afternoon in the Northwest—cold and rainy—and I was on my front porch with my young daughter, sprinkling homemade magical glitter oats along the path for Santa's reindeer that night. My little girl was loving the adventure, and so was I.

Amid our fun, I looked up as an unknown SUV pulled into our driveway. To my surprise and mild discomfort, my boss—our company's CEO—got out of the car. After exchanging greetings, he knelt next to my daughter and asked, "What does your daddy want for Christmas?" Taylor said, "He wants a bike." My boss smiled, opened the back of his SUV, and pulled out a mountain bike with a bow on it.

He had called my wife in the weeks before (as he had with all of his direct reports) and asked her if there was a Christmas gift—something I really wanted—that he could get for me. To say I was grateful and impressed would be an understatement.

In the years since, I've duplicated his efforts with my own team and have received similar sentiments in return. As much as my team appreciated the experience, though, I found that I loved the style of leadership even more.

The term "servant leader" was first coined by Robert Greenleaf in a 1970 essay, and it describes leaders who serve first, accepting that true leadership will be the result.

As the years have gone by, I've become convinced of this approach. I believe in the concept because I've experienced its effectiveness from both sides of the equation.

Looking to try the approach for yourself? Here are four quick ways to begin:

1. Learn Something Specific and Important about Every Person You Lead

There's a writing tip I love called "naming the dog." Calling the dog Sparky instead of just "the dog" makes a significant difference. Why? Because the specificity creates connotation, context, and nuance—all important factors in writing well.

Specificity in servant leadership is also important. Knowing personalized details of those you lead, especially those who show personal motivation, can make a big difference.

For example, I work with someone who, when told to do something in a very specific way, creates a situation that nearly forces him to go in the other direction. He's important to our team, and knowing this about his character, I try hard never to issue him any direction or feedback in a hyper-authoritative or declarative manner. To another person on my team who craves specific instruction, this approach would be frustrating. The key is to know those you lead specifically so you can serve them best.

2. Take Action Yourself, and Let the Credit Go Somewhere Else

Seth Godin's book *Poke the Box* examines the need for starters in organizations—the people who take initiative even when they don't have an edict to do so. According to Godin, initiative is the birthplace and differentiator of today's workplace leadership.

There are many reasons people fail to start something new or act now, but one of the biggest is a desire for credit (or, conversely, to avoid blame). Godin's solution? Give the credit away. Worry about taking action, and use the positive results as a gift for those you lead. It may seem counterintuitive, but this is the heart of servant leadership: as you help others succeed, you become more successful yourself.

3. Find a Millennial in Your Organization to Work Alongside

I work with a lot of people who are in the first or second jobs of their careers, and I'm learning so much from them. For example, many in this group prioritize the sharing of unique experiences over career advancement. It's a part of the ethos these younger workers exude, and I find it inspiring.

When you get interested in your employees and what matters to them specifically, you open the door to leading them. When you take the approach of a servant leader with the millennial generation, they will respond.

4. Commit and Believe

Traditionalists might argue that leadership is all about issuing orders with clarity and fairness. I don't believe that anymore. I believe it's more about showing people what they're capable of, mapping that to your company's direction, then letting them go to work.

It might seem counterintuitive because it cedes some perceived control. But in the end, it produces greater results. It's a philosophical investment, requiring a commitment and belief that the payoff will come. In my years of servant leadership, I've seen it pay off in spades.

In the end, the servant leader—the one who knows the troops on a deeper level—truly wins. As Greenleaf himself has said, "The difference manifests itself in the care taken by the servant first to make sure that other people's highest priority needs are being served." The best, and most difficult, test to administer is: do those served grow as people?

THAT TIME BILL GATES ANSWERED A TECH SUPPORT CALL AND CRUSHED IT

Gene Marks

"Hello, this is Microsoft Product Support, William speaking. How can I help you?"

That's exactly what he said, and it's kind of a famous story in Microsoft lore. It's worth retelling if you haven't heard it.

In 1989, Microsoft wasn't the monolith that it is today, but it was still a huge company with more than $800 million in sales and 4,000 employees. During that year, Steve Ballmer was promoted to senior vice president, the company released its flagship database SQL server and Microsoft Word 5.0 for MS-DOS, and they started selling Office for the Macintosh. The company had opened a 49,000-square-foot support center the year before and recently started a new comprehensive software support service called OnLine Plus that gave its senior support staff access to an extensive database of product information.

It was also the year that Bill Gates—famous, feared, hated, and loved—answered a tech support call.

When touring the new support facility in November of that year, he asked one of the support technicians answering the phones if he, the celebrity-CEO, could take a call. He sat down, put on a headset, and got to work. Calling himself "William" (for obvious reasons), Gates talked to the unknowing customer, collected the details, searched the company's new product support database, found the solution, and patiently walked the customer through the problem, wrapping up the call with "thank you for using Microsoft products."

How good a job did he do? Apparently, he crushed it. According to a blog post on the company's website about the incident, Gates was so good that when the customer called back later with a follow-up question, he asked again for that "nice man named

William who straightened it all out." When informed that his tech support question was answered by none other than Bill Gates himself, the customer's response was "Oh, my God."

Yeah, I get it. You're a busy person. You're putting together deals, going to meetings, reviewing contracts, playing golf with that big prospect, interviewing that new hire. But, when was the last time you handled a customer service call? Could you? When did you last go in the field and work on an installation or man a machine in the plant and stamp out a new piece? Could you? When did you last make a cold call or go on a road trip to see new customers?

For me, it's been a while. Too long.

I have a client who runs an 80-person company. When a customer service representative left for maternity leave, he decided on a whim to move his office to her cubicle for the six weeks she was out. He heard the complaints, he eavesdropped on conversations, he kibitzed with the other reps, and like Bill Gates, he even took a few calls and ran down the answers all by himself.

"I learned more about my own company in those six weeks than in the five years before," he told me about the experience. More important, his employees got a chance to spend time with him, ask him questions, and get to know him better as a person. Those six weeks strengthened his relationships and changed the way he viewed his company and his people.

If the CEO of Microsoft can take a tech support call once in a while, as my client also did, shouldn't we all be doing the same?

Of course, if you are going to do this, you need to do it for the right reasons, such as connecting with needs of customers and showing your employees that you are never too big to do the day-to-day work. This is not done to show off, nor should it be a PR stunt. It is also not the same as the television series *Undercover Boss*, where the business owners went undercover to work with the employees in an effort to find wrongdoing. This is about being authentic, transparent, and humble. You will learn what is going right and where you can improve but in an honest manner. In the end, taking a page from Bill Gates' story is an incredible way to see the process from the inside. It can be a great learning experience for a business leader. In addition, such an experience can also be very motivational for the rest of the company. It's something business owners should try, especially those who feel that they are not as connected as they once were with the people who drive the company forward: the employees and the customers.

15

EIGHT WAYS TO ADVOCATE FOR YOUR TEAM'S SUCCESS

Sherrie Campbell

Success is never a one-person job. If we want our team to be successful, we must advocate for them. Advocating for others directly increases self-confidence and their ability to perform at the peak performance levels necessary to increase their success and their team's. Following are eight ways to advocate and contribute to others' success.

1. *Acknowledge.* To advocate for another, we must acknowledge their dignity, their worth,

and their value as a human being. So often, we turn people into "things." We label them as this or that and neglect to treat them as human beings. We cannot connect with a person we treat as an "it" or an "object" because we depersonalize or minimize them down to a label. To effectively advocate for others, we must work to *view* them as people of worth, interest, and significance. When we acknowledge the dignity and worth of another, we are *seeing* them. To advocate, we must acknowledge others for who they are in the world, for what they do, and to tell them why what they do and who they are matters. This creates motivation.

2. *Touch.* There is nothing more connecting than to recognize another person through appropriate physical touch, direct eye contact, and attentiveness. When we use a light touch, we tell others they are worthy, likeable, and valuable. Most people are so tied into their phones and other electronic devices that they spend less and less time engaging in face-to-face interactions. It's important to shake hands or (when in the company of someone you know will not misinterpret the gesture) hug and to have a moment of real human-to-

human interaction. When we touch another person, we advocate for them through the stimulation of the mood hormones that create bonding and trust. When touch is appropriate, we make others feel special.

3. *Advise.* To advocate for others, we have to look beyond ourselves. We must objectively listen to and observe others to determine what is in their best interest. To advocate, we must not criticize, judge, or invalidate; instead, we should focus on guiding, brainstorming, and exploring possibilities. When we operate in this way, it allows us to advise others according to their desires—not our own. Advice coming from a selfish agenda is not good advice because it is not about being of service to another; it is more about using another person to meet our own agendas. Advocating means we want and desire for people to reach for and achieve the goals *they* come up with. Advice should mirror that sentiment by giving them ideas that help them reach their goals.

4. *Support.* The most outstanding results to come from any endeavor are born from a solid foundation of feeling, and being, supported. To provide support, we need to advocate for people in three simple ways: people need to

feel heard, valued, and understood. When someone comes to us, we are not there to fix or solve their problems; we are there to hold the space for them to vent, be in fear, and/or express their more reactive or worried emotions. When in that space, we must hold the belief *for them* that all will be OK when they cannot hold that belief for themselves. Being supportive means we act as a net. We must encourage others into their own self-reflection by asking them questions that will help them find their own answers. When we do this, others feel they can be in our presence and be supported to find themselves, amidst their own imperfections without humiliation.

5. *Coach.* Great success comes from coaching others to achieve their dreams. As we contribute to others in their success, we also achieve our own. Goals are a shared experience. Think about it: every great athlete has a coach. Power lifters are able to lift heavier weights when they have a spotter. Every person driven toward success would do best to have a coach, a therapist, a mentor, or all of the above to guide and support them in living out their personal and professional goals. When we coach others, we advocate for their success, using the best

of their abilities (not ours), and from this, they develop the tough-mindedness to go out in the world and do their best. When the person or people we advocate for have missteps, they have someone in their corner to support and coach them, with improved strategies, to push them back out there to conquer their goals.

6. *Believe.* Advocating for others comes from holding a deep and genuine belief in who they are and what they are capable of achieving. When we give this, and the other person trusts our belief in them, they will live up to the beliefs we hold to show us (and themselves) they are as capable as we believe. Success doesn't come from putting another down to get them to fight to prove us wrong. Success is better sustained when we advocate for people to prove that our belief in them is real, valid, and correct. When we deeply support, believe in, and advocate for others, they become more resilient. We must advocate for people to see their talents, their skills, and their potential. Advocating for others lifts their spirts. When spirits are high, people are better able to handle stress and conflict.

7. *Expectation.* People naturally live up or down to expectations. When we hold high, reachable

expectations of others, they will reach as far and as wide as they must to live up to what we expect. High expectations covertly communicate to others that we believe in their abilities. Our expectations naturally push them out of their comfort zones, causing them to become curious about what they are capable of achieving. In advocating for others, we increase their self-belief to see the possible realities that could come from living up to what is expected of them. Their curiosity, backed by our support and belief, influences them so deeply, they naturally begin to test the edges of their fears and begin to rise above them.

8. *Reframe.* Each person suffers from differing amounts of negative self-talk. We must learn to reframe another person's negative attitude from one of self-doubt to an attitude of possibility. The most important way to advocate for others is to focus on solutions to problems rather than on all the problems with the problem. Moving forward from a problem-focused mindset only creates more problems. As we reframe someone's negative self-talk, we model new ways for them to be in a relationship with themselves. We must

advocate for them to understand that every "no" takes them closer to their "yes." In doing this, we inspire them to see the valid reasons for staying in the grind when frustrations seem to be taking over. The idea is to change their self-talk from doubt to certainty, or from negative to positive, because there is always another way to get to the same goal.

People grow in immeasurable ways when there is a community of support behind them even if it is a community of two. We must cheer people on, advocate for them, recommend them to others, and acknowledge them publicly. We all need people in our corner to advocate for our growth and success. Advocating for others has the reciprocal effect of increasing our own sense of personal well-being and levels of success.

ENTREPRENEUR VOICES SPOTLIGHT: INTERVIEW WITH JASON HABER

Before Jason Haber wrote his 2016 book, *The Business of Good,* he sold a real estate firm, one from which each completed deal also funded the construction of a clean-water well in a developing part of the world. Haber, who has remained active in the New York real estate market, believes that social entrepreneurship should be inherent in any business enterprise. He illustrates such principles in his book with historical and current examples and anecdotes.

It should be noted that businesses that are socially responsible are also often those that have a servant leadership culture, whereby the leaders are serving the people. There are commonalities that start with leaders not putting themselves or the bottom line ahead of what is best for the people and / or the community at large. They present leadership as examples for people to follow.

In an interview with Haber, we began by asking him how the book came to fruition.

Jason Haber: I wanted to write the book, having gone through the process of starting my own entrepreneurial firm from scratch. We had no office, no clients, nothing . . . we started in my living room. It took about four years to build a company that we were able to sell. It was during that time that I learned a lot and read a lot of "what" books, which were biographical—mostly profiles that explained "what" social entrepreneurs had done, which was all well and good. But I wanted to write a "why" book that talked about "why" we do the good things we do in business.

Entrepreneur: How did you find the businesses that you included in the book—ones that answered the question, "why"?

Haber: I looked at the narrative I was constructing, did a lot of research, and had interviews with people from a lot of businesses. When I started narrowing it down to certain companies I wanted to discuss, I saw that the common thread was that social entrepreneurship was in their DNA. The idea or business of doing good was in their core—they wouldn't be in business if they weren't doing this from the start.

Entrepreneur: From a leadership perspective, are there characteristics that you see in social entrepreneurship?

Haber: Definitely. For example, you have to surround yourself with good people that you can trust. Being a good leader means understanding that you don't have to do everything. Good leaders don't do everything. They lead by example and do certain things very well. The leader is going to set the tone and set how we get to "why." Then, it's up to the team to see that same vision. I also noticed that the mark of a good leader is having people who have been around them for a long time—leaders who have a revolving door of people—are not usually good leaders. People who understand the "why" do not pick up and leave, and such leaders encourage them to stay through their commitment to social entrepreneurship.

Entrepreneur: You have a passion for history. Was there anything or anyone that inspired you as you became a leader?

Haber: I know it's a bit cliché, but I'd say Abraham Lincoln, and I'll give you a very good reason. Lincoln got elected to preserve the union. He came into office with no interest in emancipation. Then, once he was in office and saw what was going on around him, he decided not to preserve the union but instead to remake it. He left himself with the flexibility to change his position. Really good leaders can learn from that and be flexible. One of the worst things a leader can do is be so rigid that they cannot adapt to changing times, and today, things change more rapidly than ever. So a leader needs to be nimble enough to adapt to the world around them.

Entrepreneur: Beyond the book, how can you spread the business of good and the "why"?

Haber: I'm out there speaking as a keynote and at colleges. I talk about the business of good and how various techniques can be used by businesses, nonprofits, philanthropic organizations, charities, millennials, and so forth so they can learn how to be part of the good.

16

FIVE THINGS THE BEST LEADERS DO EVERY DAY

Heather R. Huhman

" Who got caught being awesome?" That's the question Alex Charfen, CEO of Austin, Texas-based training and business consultancy, asks his employees every morning at 9:17 A.M., during their daily huddle.

Charfen started this practice because he recognized that like at other rapidly growing companies, his employees weren't being properly recognized for their hard work and achievements.

Rather than sit back and wait for the issue to resolve itself, he and his team made sure that every "awesome" employee felt appreciated.

"This allows everyone, from managers to first-time employees, to publicly call out individuals for exceptional service, delivery, or mentorship," Charfen told me. "Making this a daily occurrence puts our team in a service mentality, shifting their mindset to think positively about how we interact with each other, our partners, and our clients."

To shape successful workplaces, company leaders like Charfen believe their daily culture should reflect the positive efforts employees make every day. In return, those employees become engaged, motivated, and productive.

Need more ideas to perfect your company culture? Here are five other ways to become a leader employees admire:

1. Praise Often—and in Public

Most leaders understand the importance of employees, but only the best openly show their appreciation.

Employees aren't seeking handouts in expensive gifts but rather want to know how leaders see their hard work and determination. In fact, a January

2017 survey by OfficeVibe found that 82 percent of participating employees said they thought of recognition/praise as better than a gift.

After hearing employees speak highly of spouses' employers who publicly praise employees, Stephen Twomey, founder of Traverse City, Michigan-based digital branding company MasterMindSEO, took the hint and applied it to his own company culture. Twomey says he finds one thing employees did exceptionally well the previous day or week and praises them in public for their work. Engaging his team with different forms of praise keeps everyone inspired and motivated. "Sometimes, it's in a group email, a shout-out on our social media, or a simple high five that everyone can see.

"Work productivity has increased by 30 percent," claims Twomey, adding, "I don't hear grumbling about being underappreciated, and no one is asking for a raise like they normally would around the beginning of the year. It turns out, people really want to be inspired and led—not managed."

2. Send Employees Out with a Road Map

Effective communication and motivation go hand in hand. Employees who are unsure about their daily tasks rarely get the opportunity to go above and beyond. If their everyday tasks are unclear, how can they focus on improving them?

Ensuring employees are on the same page and know they're part of a team boosts company morale and productivity. That's why Jordan Scheltgen, cofounder and managing partner of content marketing company Cave Social, in Los Angeles, opens every day with a new process to help employees focus and achieve their goals.

"We started a program we call Attack the Day," he explained to me. "This is both a mindset and process. It starts with a 20-minute meeting every morning. Teams break off and list what they want to get accomplished for the day. Then, team members are encouraged to jump in and offer assistance to other staff members on tasks they can provide value on."

3. Capture Feedback—and Actually Use It

Keeping track of employees' feelings—especially when one of them is frustrated—is a difficult task. This is an even bigger challenge to tackle as businesses and technology expand. However, without attempting to understand your employees' feedback, your ability to retain employees and improve your company processes may become nearly impossible.

During a time of rapid growth at his own business, Benjamin Snyers, managing director and partner at New York City-based social agency Social Lab, knew he needed to keep a close eye his team members' weekly pulse. Using Butterfly, a personal management coach, Snyers said he discovered his team was feeling stressed and overworked. As a result, he formally communicated his gratitude to his team members for their hard work, recognized their sacrifices, and explained why their efforts were not in vain.

After hearing feedback from employees and actively listening, Snyers said he understood his team's frustrations and was able to show them that the company leadership was 100 percent behind them.

4. Cultivate a Positive Workplace Culture

Motivating employees to reach the height of their potential is every leader's job. Addressing motivational issues only once every quarter—or worse, once a year—drains employees' productivity and passion for their role.

At advertising and marketing agency Gavin Advertising in York, Pennsylvania, CEO Mandy Arnold empowers and engages employees every day by creating a positive workplace culture. "We incorporated 'We Culture' team shout-outs," she told me. "Every Monday, we take five minutes for teammates to thank someone—out loud—for doing a great job. It could be a nod to the effort behind a great media placement secured or an SEO specialist who went above and beyond to solve a client issue on a tight timeline."

Frequent positive reinforcement, like the kind Arnold implements in her culture, brings out the best in employees. So, ensure the best talent stays and grows at your company by proving to your employees that their company leaders are invested in bringing the team together and helping them reach their greatest potential.

5. Ask for Feedback—and Prepare to Be Surprised

Miscommunication doesn't happen solely when employees don't understand a leader's expectations. It also happens, and leaves a lasting negative impact, when leaders aren't fully aware of employees' needs.

After feeling he wasn't performing at his best, motivational speaker Sean Douglas of Goldsboro, North Carolina, realized he was giving employees feedback but wasn't asking for it in return.

"I decided to ask for their feedback, and I was very surprised by their response," Douglas said. "I thought I was awesome but was actually lacking in some areas. Now, I am personable with them. I ask for their needs, and I also ask for feedback on how I'm doing as a leader and mentor."

Understanding what his team needs gives him the ability to lead according to their strengths, Douglas said. When leaders push their own opinions and agendas aside, they make room for their team to reach full potential.

17

FOUR WAYS TO REINVENT YOURSELF AFTER HITTING ROCK BOTTOM

Calvin Wayman

Entrepreneurship is a thrilling roller coaster ride. There are highs, but there are also lows. What isn't talked about enough is the struggle that so many entrepreneurs face pursuing success. How do you navigate through the tough times? Where do you turn?

What do you do when you hit rock bottom?

I sat down with entrepreneur David Schloss to learn just that. David Schloss' expertise is Facebook advertising. But in 2014, at age 25, he nearly became completely irrelevant. It had been a tough year. Things weren't clicking. On Halloween that year, David had zero dollars in his bank account. He was only 72 hours away from either coming up with his rent payment or getting kicked out. His car was two weeks away from getting impounded. It felt like walls were closing in. His business was crumbling. In this period of confusion, anxiety, self-doubt, and worry, David was a single decision away from committing career suicide and going back to a 9-to-5 job.

Thankfully for David, he turned things around. He didn't go back to being an employee. Instead, he navigated through the tough time and today is the proud owner of a successful and thriving company. What changed? How did he break through? How did he get up from his rock bottom? Here are four keys entrepreneurs can use to make it through the tough time, get back on track, and rise up in business and life.

1. Let Yourself Be Vulnerable

Sometimes, we hit walls. We struggle. Sometimes, we lose. Too often as entrepreneurs, we hide those struggles. The problem is that if you don't let yourself be real and vulnerable when you're struggling, you will hold yourself back from progressing through the tough time.

In David's period of uncertainty, being vulnerable proved to be a powerful key in his turnaround. David had hundreds of business friends on Facebook. Realizing he needed help, David reached out to every one of them for advice and guidance. Two things happened. First, he discovered that he wasn't alone——many other entrepreneurs had gone through similar things. That helped him develop confidence that he could get through it, too. Second, they gave him actionable advice to get on the right track.

Had David stayed closed up, he wouldn't have had the support he needed from others to help him move forward. When you're in a tough spot, don't be afraid to ask for help. Sharing the struggle is the bravest thing you can do. Being vulnerable isn't a sign of weakness; it's a sign of strength.

2. Develop a Vision

Ask yourself, "What do I want to create?"

It's difficult to know if you're progressing when you don't know where you're going. Stephen Covey, in *7 Habits of Highly Successful People*, writes about beginning with the end in mind. Know where you want to end up at the beginning of the trip. Reverse engineer what you want to do and where you want to go. That will become your North Star guiding your direction.

David developed a vision for the future he wanted to create. He used the advice from his colleagues to help him get super clear on his vision and direction. It's that vision that got him out of bed in the morning and motivated his work.

Vision is critical. If you don't know where you're going, how will you know when you get there?

3. Create an Action Plan

Vision is where you're going; action is what gets you there. You've heard "if you fail to plan, you plan to fail." While that's true, there's an important distinction to be made—your plan must be based on action instead of on results.

In my first book, *Fish Out of Water*, I explain how successful "sharks" focus on what's inside their control vs. outside their control. While the result is not always within your control, action is.

David got clear on where he wanted to go, then made a daily, weekly, monthly, and quarterly plan of action of how he was going to get there. To him, success wasn't based on the amount of money he made; it was based on the actions he took to make that money. He believed that if he took the right actions, results would come as a byproduct—and they did.

Decide what you want, then focus on the thing you can control to get there. Focus on action.

4. Persist

It's no surprise that things don't always go the way we planned. Persistence is a decision to keep moving toward the vision no matter what hiccups occur along the way. It's not just doing what it takes. It's doing whatever it takes. It's falling and getting up again. Life is like a chess game. You create a plan and a strategy, but how you win will not be the exact way you planned. Why? There are many unknown variables. It's continuing to take the action and not turn back.

Things didn't abruptly become sunshine and roses while David was in the day-to-day grind, but he persisted no matter what. That's why he is where he is today. Planning is what gets you moving; persistence is what keeps you going.

Entrepreneurship is an exciting adventure and a fulfilling journey—not just a satisfying destination.

It's not just about where we are going but who we become throughout the process. David began to realize he wasn't the same person anymore. He was changing. It was like he was a butterfly now, and while he didn't know it at the time, the low point forced his metamorphosis.

As I talked about in a podcast interview, it's often the struggle that turns us into great entrepreneurs. So just remember: when you're in a tough spot, it only means you're being reborn into the new you. The exciting question is: what will your metamorphosis look like?

HOW TO MOTIVATE YOUR TEAM MEMBERS BY PUTTING THEIR NEEDS FIRST

Jennifer Biry

Leadership styles are like fingerprints. They leave an unmistakable mark on whatever they touch and are unique to each individual. And while we don't get to choose our fingerprints, we do get to choose how we lead those around us.

I've had the opportunity to see a wide variety of leadership styles. I gained most of my experience working at large corporations, but for 20 years, I've been married to an entrepreneur who showed me the challenges that come with running your own business. I've learned that no matter the size of your organization or the scope of your role at work, you can be a leader. But deciding which leadership style is right for you takes time.

For me, servant leadership has proved to be the most effective approach.

Here are five steps you can take to be a servant leader.

1. Be Humble

Ego plays a huge role in your leadership style. I believe confidence balanced with humility is a recipe for leadership success. Don't let personal pride get in the way of trying something new. Always assume someone in the room is smarter than you. You'll learn more that way.

I see this kind of humility on a regular basis from Cynt Marshall, former chief diversity officer of AT&T. She has an incredibly demanding job that requires a significant investment of time for all her internal and external commitments. But when you talk to her, she gives you 100 percent of her attention and makes it clear that you're her number-one priority at that moment. She constantly uplifts her team by celebrating their great work, and she goes out of her way to make them look good. As a result, people follow her without question.

2. Trust Your Team

In most cases, you hired the people on your team because you were confident in their abilities. Trust your intuition, and give up a little control. Creativity flourishes in an open environment, so don't constrict your employees by involving yourself in smaller decisions that they can handle. Giving your team room to grow will benefit everyone in the long run.

I was on the receiving end of this kind of trust when I was a CFO supporting AT&T's call centers. Our boss tasked us with trying to figure out how to reduce the number of customer transfers between the centers. After a week of analyzing procedures, we put forth our recommendation. At the end of our presentation, our boss told us he knew a solution from the get-go; he just wanted to hear the ideas we came up with when we worked as a team to solve the problem. He was pleased to find that we uncovered other possibilities he hadn't yet considered. Encouraging us to have ownership over the solution was a powerful example for me of what it means to truly trust your team.

3. Lead from the Back of the Room

If you're a supervisor, don't think you need to be front and center all the time. It's important to listen intently—at least twice as often as you speak. Create an environment where all voices and ideas are heard, and most important, give your team room to spread their wings. For example, if they did the work, they should present the results.

By doing this, you can serve as your employees' guide instead of dictating their every move. Let the team lead themselves, and be willing to accept mistakes or failures. This will encourage risk-taking and help your employees learn how to manage similar challenges in the future.

4. Set a Broad Vision

Servant leadership isn't about being the nice guy; it's about delivering great results. Anyone who's worked with me will tell you I have high standards and push my team to excel. However, instead of managing each task, I inspire my team by helping them see that what they do is a critical component of a greater cause. Over the years, I found that people will work even harder if they believe in what they're doing.

Many times in my career, I've been asked to lead cost-cutting projects. As you might imagine, those aren't the most popular assignments to work on. So, I always try to create a broader vision. As opposed to tasking my team with cutting costs, I ask that they look for ways to increase earnings per share enough to elevate the stock price. People are always more motivated by seeing the impact of their work on a broader scale.

5. Develop Future Leaders

One of my most important responsibilities is to develop the next generation of leaders. As it turns out, it's also what I enjoy most about my job. When I mentor someone, I ask them in return to pull five more leaders forward with them. If you don't have a mentoring program in your organization, set one up. Your employees will develop stronger relationships and share insights and skills. And the emphasis you put on their professional growth will make them feel more valued.

Practicing these behaviors will bolster your team's success and foster an environment of respect across your organization. You'll be seen as a leader, not as a boss.

Take some time to step back, assess your leadership style, and look for ways to improve. Is there room for more humility? Can you relinquish some control? And are you personally invested in every employee's success?

Ask yourself these questions, and then make it a priority to empower your team. Once you start "walking the walk" of servant leadership, you'll see your people shine.

PART III
LEADING FROM THE BOTTOM UP— REFLECTIONS

Bill Gates taking a customer service call, a leader asking, "Who got caught being awesome?" and other leaders taking on the humble servant-leader approach is what makes bottom-up leadership work. Contrary to the critics, it doesn't mean such leaders are lacking in strength; it means they are lacking the need for ongoing bravado and praise, which is often the Achilles' heel of autocratic leaders.

Real strength means leading from the back of the room, letting others take the praise, asking for feedback from everyone in the company, learning from anyone and everyone, and making those who spend their days working in your company feel acknowledged, respected, and empowered. It's not about them being honored to have the opportunity to work for you; it's about you being honored to have such employees.

This is not to say that leaders must make a firm decision between top-down and bottom-up styles of leadership. Companies like Toyota use both, while other businesses incorporate aspects of each style depending on needs of the company. A former owner of a major airlines parts manufacturing company made sure to acknowledge all employees while walking around and talking with them, and by personally signing and sending birthday cards to everyone, even when there were 600 employees. He would hand over tasks and let people run with them, taking a cue from Walt Disney, who said, "At the moment of truth, every single employee can make a decision on behalf of the customer." This type of empowerment only occurs if you, as an owner, can relinquish some level of control. However, there were still areas of the business in which he felt he had to maintain more overall control—after all, the business literally started in his basement.

Bottom-up leadership is gaining greater acceptance. It needs to be well-organized, managed carefully, transparent, and all-inclusive to be most successful. And it requires leaders who do not need praise but will instead be fulfilled when their teams receive praise.

LEADING TO SUCCESS

t's hard to reach success if you don't know what it looks like. Success for the leader of a nonprofit, a family-run business, a rapidly growing tech startup, or a fortune 500 company may look very different. However, they all have something in common: a vision of the future. To get there, they set pre-determined goals. After all, you could never score a touchdown if there was no end zone—consider that every game of touch football in the park begins with someone saying, "OK, those trees are the end zone." Reaching those trees defines what success will look like.

For leaders, success is all about reaching a goal through the people they lead. Therefore, reaching success means having enlightened, engaged, involved individuals who want to buy into the goals and vision you have set forth. To do this, you need to understand where you are presently and where you want to be. Quite frankly, leading means going from point A to point B. If you are not moving your people, your business, your class, or even your constituents forward in some manner, you are not leading.

Leading successfully also means trusting other people. If you don't trust anyone, you'll end up doing everything yourself or worse, micromanaging everyone. This does not bode well for success in any business. Therefore, even if reaching your goal means taking an occasional step back now and then, it's worthwhile in the long run. Trusting your people to handle tasks, spearhead projects, and make decisions, even though they will make mistakes along the way, will boost the confidence of the people you are leading. The more confident and engaged they are, the more they will contribute to your company's success. Also, trusting and empowering people by delegating responsibilities frees you up to do the things you excel at, which further leads to success.

The bottom line is that success as a leader starts by having a vision, a goal, and a plan to get there. You will then need to trust and rely on your team to make success happen. It helps if you stay at the top of your game. The most successful leaders remain current and active mentally and physically. They seek knowledge and absorb as much as they can, take occasional risks, stay fit, get enough sleep, and make time to step away from the daily grind to enjoy and appreciate life.

HOW ONE EXECUTIVE BECAME A TRANSFORMATIONAL LEADER

Matt Mayberry

In every organization, regardless of size or industry, success rises and falls with leadership. Sure, an organization with average leadership can experience some success, but the longevity of that success and growth will be drastically shortened compared to that of an organization with a transformational leader.

So, what is a transformational leader?

In my own view, transformational leaders not only build incredible organizations that grow every year, but also they inspire their people to constantly innovate and reach their full potential.

Transformational leaders create an extraordinary vision for their organizations, one which employees are eager to buy into and work incredibly hard for every day to bring it to life. What's more, transformational leaders are obsessed with developing their people—not just collecting a profit.

To put it simply, transformational leaders positively disrupt individual organizations and entire industries.

In a March 2009 article in *Psychology Today*, Ronald Riggio writes

> "Research evidence clearly shows that groups led by transformational leaders have higher levels of performance and satisfaction than groups led by other types of leaders. Why? Because transformational leaders hold positive expectations for followers, believing that they can do their best.
>
> "As a result, they inspire, empower, and stimulate followers to exceed normal levels of performance. And transformational leaders focus on and care about followers and their personal needs and development."

I recently had the pleasure of spending the day with Bill Darcy, CEO of the National Kitchen & Bath Association. Darcy has not only transformed an organization but an entire industry. Darcy is a transformational leader through and through. When you speak to his employees or colleagues at different companies, the impact and influence he has had is clear.

In our conversation, Darcy and I discussed three factors that have helped him rise to the top and become the transformational leader he is today.

1. Make Each Day Count

Spending the entire day with Darcy, I could easily see that he truly lived every day to the fullest. It's not a coincidence that he listed this as number one when I asked him the three most important things that helped him get to where he is today.

Darcy mentioned that he learned the importance of making each day count when his son was born with a rare congenital abnormality, and it was unclear whether the boy was going to make it or not. "Going through the experience of nearly losing my son changed not only my life forever, but also how I work and lead on a daily basis," said Darcy.

Transformational leaders, in short, don't waste their days. They make every single day count, and it shows in everything they do. They possess an incredible sense of urgency, which inspires their team members to act in the same manner. As legendary basketball coach John Wooden once said, "Make each day your masterpiece."

2. Perseverance Is Key

If you dig deep into the backstory of any transformational leader to analyze this person's path to where they are today, you will often notice an incredible level of perseverance. Leaders, like anyone, experience plenty of tough and challenging times. Transformational leaders, however, stay poised during these times and trust in their process to get the job done.

Darcy said, "I have been rejected in my career more times than I can count, but the one thing that I always stayed true to was to keep fighting for what you believe in. When you keep fighting, breakthroughs eventually arise."

3. Effort Equals Results

At the young age of 25, Darcy was working for the billionaire and Penske Corp. chairman, Roger Penske. Penske instilled in his organization, and all his employees, the slogan "Effort equals results," and Darcy told me that he was able to see firsthand how vital those words were in the company's growth and success.

"Every detail mattered, and the slogan that Penske used created a huge cultural influence," Darcy said. "No one ever had to guess what was expected of them when they showed up to work in the morning.

"As a leader, you set the tone within your organization," Darcy added. "The one thing that we can all control when we show up to work is the effort that we put forth."

I hope Darcy's story of becoming a transformational leader inspires you to have the same kind of influence on not only the organization that you lead but the entire industry you are in.

20

BEING A TRUSTED LEADER: KNOWING HOW TO GROW YOUR COMPANY

Heather R. Huhman

The family-like environment of a new business can be a powerful thing. It allows both employees and leaders to come into work each day feeling as though they're there to make a difference. By being a team, employees feel the company is stronger.

"When I first started Overit, it was just a small marketing agency," recalls Dan Dinsmore, founder and CEO of Overit, in Albany, New York. "I was involved in everything and got to interact with employees on a daily basis."

But as startups begin to evolve, that relationship may be hard to maintain, as Dinsmore discovered. To take his company to the next level, he needed to hire middle managers to oversee operations. Doing that, however, created a distinct divide between him and his employees.

"It started to feel like an 'us vs. them' environment," Dinsmore pointed out. "That wasn't the kind of company I wanted to build."

To get things back on track, Dinsmore said he needed to rethink his company and how he could once again be a trusted leader. It took a lot of work to rebuild a culture of transparency and honesty.

Luckily, it's possible to avoid that "us vs. them" mentality. Here are four strategies for keeping your startup employees and leadership united:

1. Admit Your Mistakes

One of the hardest things for leaders to do is to own up when they are wrong. The feeling is that any mistake will be viewed as weakness or incompetence. But to be a trusted leader, being accountable for failure is a necessity.

"Right out of college, I was an assistant receptionist for a big-time entertainment executive in New York," recalled Kirsten Helvey, now the COO of Cornerstone OnDemand in Santa Monica, California. "One day, I got his lunch order wrong."

It wasn't long before Helvey's boss called her and screamed at her for the mistake. Despite the fact that any of his other assistants could have corrected the issue, he wanted to make sure she knew she'd messed up. "At that point," Helvey went on to say, "All trust was broken: his trust in my ability as his assistant and mine in his temperament as a manager."

Luckily, her boss had a change of heart. About 30 minutes later, he called Helvey back. He apologized for his behavior and said there was no excuse to speak to her that way. The incident turned into a life lesson Helvey uses now that she's part of the C-suite.

"It showed me that even if you're at the top, you can still mess up and damage the trust between you and your employees. But if you hold yourself accountable and make amends to the people your mistake has impacted, you can recover, grow, and even strengthen that relationship."

2. Delegate

As a leader, you may find it difficult to let go of control of any aspect of your company. But to be a trusted leader, being able to delegate is a must.

Otherwise, employees may doubt their leader's capabilities.

"When I first hired employees for my small business, I found that it was challenging for me to let go of certain tasks and trust that my employees could handle them," said Rachel Beider, CEO and founder of Massage Williamsburg and Massage Greenpoint, in New York City. "I was used to doing everything myself and at a certain standard."

However, it wasn't long before her micromanaging began to take a toll. "I think it drove everyone a little crazy at first," Beider said. "We weren't being as productive as we should have been at that time."

Once she decided to take a step back, however, things began to run more smoothly. Her employees began to feel trusted, and she was able to concentrate on the company's growth and long-term goals.

To make delegating easier, take a moment and think: is there anyone else who can successfully do this task? If the answer is yes, pass it on to that person and focus on big-picture strategies.

3. Empower Your Employees to Ask for Feedback

Things move fast at a growing startup. There is always something to do, and sometimes, providing employees with feedback gets overlooked. But that causes them to feel forgotten by their leaders.

After working in a fast-paced company following college, Steffen Maier soon learned this lesson firsthand. Whenever his manager found time to give him feedback, months had typically passed since the project was completed. This time gap left him unsure of his own personal career progress.

"The interesting thing is that after I left my job to pursue a master's degree in strategic entrepreneurship, I was surprised to find that many of my peers had faced similar experiences," said Maier, now the cofounder of Impraise in New York City.

As a result, he and a few others teamed up to create Impraise, a platform designed to make it easy for employees to ask for and receive feedback. Using this or similar tools allows employees to continue to feel supported and connected with trusted leaders.

4. Put Trust Above All Else

Never forget that a huge part of organizational trust is communication and honesty—without them, employees find it impossible to know where they stand. And that creates a division between those in the know and those who aren't.

"For us, success begins with trust," said Tom Morselli, senior vice president of people operations at PulsePoint, a programmatic advertising technology company based in New York City. "Trust in our leadership, trust in our mission, and trust among the team. It takes hard work and must be earned by 'walking the walk,' keeping promises, following through, and aligning one's leadership style with the company's core values."

All of that happens through clear and consistent communication at all levels of the company. Luckily, there are multiple, easy-to-use tools that help keep teams connected. One option is Simpplr, a platform that offers organizations an intranet that promotes and maintains productive information-sharing. It gives employees access to company news and a way to formally and informally interact with one other.

Employees should also recognize, however, that all that talk needs a follow-up.

"The most empathetic and best-intended talk is hollow if it isn't followed by action," Morselli pointed out. "Trust erodes quickly if you consistently fail to meet your commitments."

21

FIVE LEADERSHIP LESSONS ON THE COURT FOR BUSINESS OFF THE COURT

Jeff Hayzlett

Each year in March, more than 50 million Americans seem more interested in their brackets and office pools than in their work.

March Madness is the season that spurs sports fans to become glued to their TVs and mobile devices as they constantly check how their favorite college basketball team is faring.

Moreover, March Madness is when the entire nation seemingly comes to a standstill. Estimates are that during the first week of the tournament, employers may be losing nearly $4 billion in revenue. While those figures may seem astronomical, all is not lost.

How's that? Because the tournament can still teach everyone a few things about business.

March Madness has been examined in terms of the business lessons the tourney offers in numerous publications looking to cash in on the mega popularity that accompanies the annual event. But you can add a twist—a gender twist—by exploring the lessons that can be learned from the University of Connecticut (UConn) women's basketball team.

You don't have to be a basketball fiend to have heard about UConn's women's basketball team. The Huskies have been a basketball powerhouse for over 20 years. Indeed, their 111 consecutive wins will stand tall for many years to come.

The Huskies have been led by Auriemma for 32 years. His impressive resume includes an unbelievable win-loss record of 991 to 135 for the 2016-2017 season, with 11 national titles, 18 Final Four appearances, 6 perfect seasons, and 43 Conference titles. How has Coach Auriemma been able to achieve such a high level of success? He's done this by creating a culture where every player is accountable and where players may have the odds stacked against them but are empowered to figure things out on their own and worry about potential consequences later.

Here are five leadership lessons that entrepreneurs can take away from UConn's success.

1. Become a People Person and Know Your Team's Capabilities

Coach Auriemma has said, "I don't hire good coaches; I hire good people. If they turn out to be good coaches, too, that's a plus." A good coach, or leader, is an essential tool for success. Many have described Auriemma as a taskmaster, but he has also been described by rival coaches as a people person.

Being a people person doesn't mean you have to like everyone you work with. It means that as a leader you need to make an effort to understand what motivates each individual on the team and harness that power to push them toward excellence. A good leader strives to move the needle forward and then gets everyone on the team to use the same playbook and execute the same play. Personal success? It's directly tied into the team's success.

A true leader knows what the entire team is capable of.

2. Put the Pedal to the Metal

Coach Auriemma's practices are known for their high-octane intensity as each practice is harder and more intense than the one before. Auriemma ups the ante so his players learn to thrive in high-pressure environments, look for solutions to problems on their own, and become mentally tougher.

For example, he makes players run "break the press" drills, meaning trying to get the ball up court against a very tough defense. They run the practice with mostly male players. He always wants the players to figure out how to get out of a tough situation.

If a player isn't mentally tough enough to handle this constant pressure during practice, she is probably not going to get into the game much and probably won't be on the team much longer, either.

In business, employers similarly should always up the ante—not to frustrate their entire staff, but to look for ways to challenge them to always be quick on their feet, nimble in high-pressure situations, and aim to exceed expectations.

Leaders, as well, should empower their team to act on their instincts and industry expertise without constantly asking for approval. A good leader gives employees the right tools to think and act for themselves and worries about consequences later.

3. Own Your Mistakes

Auriemma is a self-described hard-ass. He recruits athletes who are mentally tough, have a team mentality, and will stop at nothing to win a championship. He's said, "If you accept mistakes because it's a game . . . then as you go on in the rest of your life and the stakes get higher and things get tougher, the only thing you learned is how to make mistakes and excuses."

"Excuses are like a-holes," I wrote in my book, *Think Big, Act Bigger*. Excuses are easy, addictive, and designed to shut things down. I see them as self-imposed obstacles that prevent us from reaching our full potential. There's always a reason not to do something or an explanation for why something didn't happen.

Own your mistakes and avoid excuses. No one wants to hear them.

4. Set Realistic Goals

No matter how much experience you have or how big a star you think you are, you always have something to learn. Young players arrive in Connecticut knowing that their odds of their cracking the starting lineup are almost nil. But they also know they're at the right place to elevate their game, maybe become part of the starting lineup, and even win a championship or two.

It's the same in a business setting. You may have 30 years of experience, but there's always something that you might not know or fully understand. So, what now? The answer: become an expert at as many things as possible. It's OK for you as leader not to have a full understanding of a specific topic, but if you want people to follow you and look up to you, you have to study the topic, learn it, and master it to become that expert.

I don't know a single person who knows everything, but I know plenty of people who spend hours learning a new task to perfect it and gain an edge professionally.

5. Have a Back-Up Plan, Always

How many times have we seen a play break down during a game? We've seen plenty of coaches lose their marbles on the sidelines because a player failed to execute a play the way it was drawn up. Sometimes, that breakdown costs the team the game.

Coach Auriemma, for one, has a wide variety of plays for each phase of the tournament. He's known for drawing up three different ways to start each play, in case Plan A breaks down.

If you are trying to draw new business, impress an existing client with your strategy, or simply conduct day-to-day business, know that nothing is ever perfect. Sometimes, the variants are minimal, and sometimes, they are monumental. But if you don't prepare for each situation, you'll lose the game. And preparation means having a Plan B and even C.

In the end, practicing at game speed for every possible scenario, and preparing for every possible variable, will be what helps you win the game. Preparation is key—during March Madness, in business, and in life.

HOW TO LEAD VS. MANAGE YOUR TEAM'S SUCCESS

Bob Glazer

It takes great leaders and talent to grow a successful company. One of the best descriptions of a leader I've heard is that leaders focus on vision and strategy, guiding and removing obstacles for their teams—something like a coach in sports.

Managers typically focus more on the execution piece: working in the business. By contrast, real leadership means providing a compelling vision and clear direction. Successful leaders clarify priorities and expectations, defining employee roles and ensuring that the processes and capacities required for them to execute are in place.

The stance from which you lead makes a big difference in your employees' job satisfaction. To engage your workers today, focus more on leading instead of managing. I've found that most employees are looking for coaches who can help them add value to the company by developing and making the most of their strengths. This is especially true when it comes to millennials, the largest generation in the work force.

Leading a productive team entails letting go of daily operations to focus on setting a clear strategy and vision—the "why" and "what"—and getting comfortable leaving your team to manage the "how." This can be a serious challenge if you're accustomed to spending most of your time triaging problems, putting out fires, and managing from a reactive standpoint.

Managers execute—leaders lead.

As the CEO of a digital marketing agency, I used to review every monthly report for quality before it went out to our clients, which involved far too much "managing" time.

Realizing it would not scale, I sat down one day and wrote a playbook on how to create these reports, trained the team, and then let them loose. I still ask to be copied on them, but now, I can focus on coaching people on opportunities to improve, and they know they won't get my feedback before they send. This approach creates more accountability for others and less doing on my part.

When I empowered the team to write those monthly reports, everyone saw better outcomes. Here are three more ways you can shift from day-to-day management to leadership.

1. Establish Core Values—and Follow Them

While 80 percent of Fortune 100 companies talk about their core values publicly, according to one study, they are often hollow words that aren't operationalized in any way. The magic of core values is that, when they are ingrained into employees' daily work lives, they drive more autonomous decision making.

For example, one of our core values is "embrace relationships," which empowers our managers to make financial decisions aligned with long-term outcomes—not short-term maximization of profits. Someone might say to me, "I made this concession for one of our partners because it was the right thing to do," rather than feel the need to ask for permission.

To create the right conditions for success and to lead by example, employees need to understand where the business is going and how they should behave. Your core values inform your company culture; including the team in creating those values can help workers feel more connected and empowered.

2. Don't Neglect Your Own Professional Development

Too often, leaders assume responsibility for everyone on their teams but themselves. Although we all need to manage at times, leaders are usually proactive; managers are reactive. If you want to be a great leader, set aside time for your own professional development.

Join local and national professional organizations, such as Entrepreneurs' Organization—a great resource for networking and leadership training—or attend conferences such as GrowCo to hear from other leaders who have found success.

Look for groups that will challenge and support you in your professional development beyond networking and handing out business cards. Seek out a successful coach or mentor, and create a formal board of advisors. Nothing is ever as easy as it looks, so lean on the support and experience of others to guide you, and learn from those who have done what you aim to do.

And don't forget to transfer this focus on development to your team. GitHub, a code hosting provider for techies, for example, allows each of its employees to attend one work-related conference a year and covers the travel costs if a teammate is invited to speak.

3. Spread the Love, or Risk Burnout

If you try to do it all yourself, you will inevitably see diminishing returns on the time you invest. Successful leaders spend the majority of their time on tasks that use their own unique skills and abilities and leave the rest to others who are more competent in those areas.

Try this exercise to figure out how to make that happen:

- Determine the maximum number of hours per week you can work and stay balanced.

- Calculate (honestly) how much time it takes to do all your necessary tasks well. If the answer is more than 100 percent of your max hours, delegate.

- List everything you do in a day.

- Create two columns to sort that list: in column one, list every task you love to do and are great at; column two is for everything else.

- Stop doing, or delegate, everything in column two that puts you over capacity.

The great thing is you'll often discover that the duties you aren't good at (or don't enjoy) align with the unique capabilities and favorite tasks of someone else on your team.

Although it might seem impossible to let go of the daily tasks of managing the business, getting out of that mindset and focusing on how to be an inspirational leader is the best investment you can make—in both your quality of life and the success of your business.

TEN BOOKS EVERY LEADER SHOULD READ TO BE SUCCESSFUL

Deep Patel

One of the best ways to ensure that you grow as a person and a leader is to read—a lot.

Time and time again, we learn that the most successful people are also avid bookworms. Constant reading allows them to absorb knowledge, broaden their worldviews and perspectives, and challenge obsolete viewpoints.

But, of course, not all books are worthy of the time and effort it takes to go from cover to cover.

To help you on your journey toward becoming a successful leader, here are the top 10 books you should be reading now.

1. *Managing the Mental Game* by Jeff Boss

Using a blend of mental-training methodologies, former Navy SEAL Jeff Boss shows readers how to build self-confidence and fortitude, enabling them to reach new levels of success.

Managing the Mental Game contains useful exercises on learning how to manage chaos and pressure in order to stay clearheaded and calm in uncertain and difficult situations. Boss' advice helps you understand that stress is a mental game that can be overcome and is overcome often by avoiding mental pitfalls and learning to replace negative thoughts with positive ones.

2. *Start with Why* by Simon Sinek

This book centers on an important business truth: people don't buy what you do, they buy why you do it. Simon Sinek explains this concept in *Start with Why* by delving into a few basic questions. One key question he poses is why some people and organizations are more innovative, influential, and profitable than others.

He also asks why so few are able to repeat their success. If you are struggling to create a long-term vision and guiding principles as you navigate business and life, this book can give you the inspiration to begin moving in the right direction.

3. *The Go-Giver Leader* by Bob Burg and John David Mann

Great leaders don't try to act like "leaders." Instead, they strive to be more human. They focus on the concept that "if you give, you shall receive." Burg and Mann tell a compelling tale of an ambitious young executive trying to lead a struggling small business to make a crucial decision.

The Go-Giver Leader promotes a mindset of higher consciousness. It expands on the idea that your influence is determined by whether you place others' interests first. Leaders who do this will create prosperity for their communities and society, as well as for their companies and employees.

4. *The Dip* by Seth Godin

The Dip proves that winners do quit, and quitters do win. Seth Godin shows that winners quit quickly and often until they commit to beating the right "dip."

Winners are those who know that the bigger the barrier, the bigger the reward for getting past it. If you can beat the dip, you'll earn profits, glory, and long-term security. What this book will do is help you determine if you're in a dip that's worthy of your time, effort, and talents.

5. *Freakonomics* by Steven Levitt and Stephen J. Dubner

As *The Wall Street Journal* proclaims, "If Indiana Jones were an economist, he'd be Steven Levitt." *Freakonomics* is a groundbreaking collaboration between Levitt and Stephen J. Dubner, an award-winning author and journalist.

The two examined the inner workings of a crack gang, the truth about real estate agents, and the secrets of the Ku Klux Klan. The result of their work is this book, which powerfully shows how, at its core, economics is the study of incentives. It is how people get what they want or need, especially when other people are trying to get the same thing.

6. *Essentialism* by Greg McKeown

Instead of trying to manage your time more efficiently, *Essentialism* helps you focus on getting the right things done. This isn't about time management or productivity improvement. Greg McKeown teaches a systematic discipline for discerning what is absolutely essential and eliminating everything else.

By pursuing "less," we are empowered to prioritize what is truly important in our lives, and thus, we are able to give the highest possible contribution toward those things.

7. *Drive* by Daniel H. Pink

We all have an innate desire to be in control of our lives and create new things. These two desires are what truly drive us. The "carrot and stick" approach that most corporations use to motivate people doesn't deliver high performance or results because it ignores the most important element: intrinsic (or internal) motivation.

Daniel H. Pink asserts in that the secret to prompting higher achieving workers is to tap into their internal motivation. Doing so will increase satisfaction at work, at school, and at home and empower us to better ourselves and our world.

8. *Getting Things Done* by David Allen

Since *Getting Things Done* was first published 15 years ago, "GTD" has become shorthand for an entire method of approaching professional and personal tasks. This updated version includes new material that adds fresh perspectives to David Allen's classic text on how to attain maximum efficiency.

Allen offers important tools and strategies on how to focus our energy and manage workflows, including how to get through work tasks quickly, delegate when appropriate, and defer when necessary.

9. *Give and Take* by Adam Grant

Success is not just about hard work, talent, and luck. Our ability to achieve is increasingly dependent on how well we interact with others. Adam Grant's book shows that most people operate as takers, matchers, or givers.

Whereas takers strive to get as much as possible from others and matchers aim to trade evenly, givers are a rare breed who contribute to others without expecting anything in return. When used correctly, giving can attain extraordinary results.

10. *What They Don't Teach You at Harvard Business School* by Mark H. McCormack

Like a wise mentor, this book offers real-world guidance and concise information that you won't learn elsewhere. *What They Don't Teach You at Harvard Business School* is a complement to a traditional business background offered by a seasoned luminary in the field.

Mark H. McCormack teaches you how to use his "applied people sense" in sales, negotiation, executive time management, and reading yourself and others.

SHOULD YOU TAKE BUSINESS ADVICE THAT CONTRADICTS YOUR INSTINCTS?

Jayson DeMers

"**G**o with your gut." It's an appealing phrase that encourages business owners, professionals, and talented individuals everywhere to stop overanalyzing a situation and instead rely on their instincts to make an important decision.

But in the business world, you'll have plenty of hard evidence, anecdotal evidence, and input from others to guide your decision making. You'll have partners, mentors, co-workers, investors, perhaps friends and family members, and even clients or customers giving you advice for the development of your business.

So, what happens when your instincts contradict a piece of advice given to you by someone, or even multiple people, you respect? Should you take their advice even if it contradicts your gut feeling?

The Case for Instinct

There's no scientific rubric that allows you to test the true power of your instincts, and many entrepreneurs trust their instincts because of some supernatural quality they ascribe to them.

This is somewhat akin to a superstition that can't be proved or disproved and may be hard to argue with. But ignoring that, here are some of the practical, logical reasons why you might be wise to trust your instincts over outside advice:

Snap Judgments

Snap judgments come from immediately responding to a situation and making a decision on how to act or react. Leaders who can quickly take in the situation, plus the surroundings, and act based on their own experiences, can make productive snap judgments.

Your "instincts," in some cases, are merely the product of your experience, your beliefs, and a high-level assessment of a given scenario. Think of it as your subconscious mind doing all the problem-solving work for you and making a reasonable estimation rather than precisely calculating the "right" answer.

Accordingly, you'll find that many of your snap judgments and decisions turn out to be correct—but only if you have the experience to back them up. For example, a novice chess player wouldn't be able to "feel" that a move is correct the same way a grandmaster would.

Mavericks

Some of the most successful businesses are those with brands that are unlike anything else on the market. They're the ones that dared to do what everyone else was afraid to and kept going, despite people telling them not to.

Following the advice of the majority will lead you down the path of the majority—to moderate, but never breakout, success. The argument here is that if you want a chance at standing out from the crowd, you have to go against the grain, at least some of the time.

Satisfaction

Don't neglect the importance of your decision's aftermath. Imagine a scenario in which, against your instincts, you followed the advice of a mentor. Ultimately, this led you down a terrible path that resulted in losing a major client. Chances are, you had a hard time forgiving yourself for not going with your gut to begin with.

But, if you make your own decision and fail, you'll at least accept responsibility for your own destiny.

The Problems Instinct May Bring

Don't let the above arguments fool you into believing that your instincts are always right. Consider the following problems:

- *Experience*. If you're a new entrepreneur, remember there are many more people who are far more experienced than you are. Your capacity for snap judgments is limited, and people wiser than you have likely been through this situation before. Remain humble in your early stages, and trust the more experienced people. You don't have to agree with them on everything, but at least listen to what they have to say.

- *Survivorship bias*. The maverick argument may be convincing, but don't forget that our view of successful entrepreneurs is affected by survivorship bias. Essentially, we only hear stories about the entrepreneurs who contradicted advice and ended up becoming millionaires—not the people who contradicted advice and became failures. Keep this in mind before you try emulating your favorite celebrity business owner.

- *Evidence and intuition.* Remember that evidence exists as an objective reality, and intuition exists as a subjective feeling. Using your feelings to contradict evidence is often unwise; for example, believing that the traffic light is green doesn't change the fact that it's red. However, in the absence of evidence, intuition can help you fill in the gaps.

- *Limitations of snap judgments.* Snap judgments may often end up being correct, but that doesn't mean they have a perfect track record. If you've ever jumped in fright after seeing a mannequin in a dimly lit room, you know this all too well.

When it comes to making a tough decision, prioritize objective information as much as you can—no amount of instinct should overrule significant and clear evidence that contradicts your gut feeling. But in cases where the "right" answer isn't clear, where evidence is fuzzy, and where you fundamentally disagree with your partners, let your instinct guide you in the right direction.

Decisiveness is more important than always making the perfect decision, so pick a direction and stick with it.

THIS FOUNDER SAYS THE WORST ADVICE CAME FROM HIS USERS

Nina Zipkin

Editor's Note: Entrepreneur's "20 Questions" series features established and up-and-coming entrepreneurs and asks them questions about what makes them tick, their everyday success strategies, and advice for aspiring founders.

If you have ever had to tell your computer that you are not a robot and type a series of words and numbers when you subscribe to an email newsletter, you've run into Luis von Ahn's work. In 2000, with his mentor Manuel Blum, he invented CAPTCHA, or Completely Automated Public Turing test to tell Computers and Humans Apart. He built two companies on the technology, which he sold to Google in 2009.

He was just about to turn 30, and he found himself at a career crossroads. "I was having sort of a quarter-life crisis, wondering what I am going to do with the rest of my life," recalled von Ahn.

So, he set his sights on a new project and wanted to do something he was passionate about. Having seen how a lack of education can impact opportunity and factor into economic disparity in his native Guatemala, and given his love for teaching as a computer science professor at his graduate alma mater, Carnegie Mellon University, education and learning seemed like a natural focus.

"My views about education are very influenced by being from Guatemala. The rich people can buy themselves the best education in the world, whereas the poor people rarely learn how to read and write, and because of that, they never make much money," von Ahn says. "I wanted to do something that would give equal access to education to everybody."

His solution to bridge that gap was to remove the time constraints and costs often attached to gaining fluency in a new language.

"There are over a billion people in the world learning a foreign language," he says. "Then I asked, 'Can we find a way for people to learn a foreign language for free?' " That's how his startup Duolingo got its start.

With Duolingo, users can choose from 27 languages, from Spanish to Swedish, and learn through small, gamified lessons. Since the company's launch in 2011, it has raised $83.3 million in funding, been awarded iPhone App of the Year in 2013, and was the Best of the Best for Android in 2013 and 2014. It is also the most downloaded app in the "Education" category on Android and iOS worldwide, and the free app has garnered 150 million users around the world, according to the company.

We caught up with von Ahn to ask him 20 questions about what makes him tick.

(This interview is edited for clarity and brevity.)

1. *How do you start your day?*

   I wake up pretty early, between 5 and 6 A.M. First thing I do is check my email, and the second thing I do is check the Duolingo metrics from the day before, like revenue and active users. I don't know if that is a good idea or not because my mood for the rest of the day is correlated to that. Then, I work out for 16 minutes. I work out at maximum speed for 16 minutes; it is a time-saving device. The working out wakes me up and gives me a lot of energy; I feel pretty refreshed after that.

2. *How do you end your day?*
That varies depending on what I did during the day. Sometimes, I just get back from a late dinner and go to bed immediately. If I have time, I try to wrap everything up before the next day so I don't have anything that carries over. That's rare, but when I am able to do that, that makes me feel a lot better. If I can start the next day with nothing immediately carrying over, that really helps me.

3. *What's a book that changed your mind?*
The Design of Everyday Things by Don Norman. Before I read that book, I didn't pay a lot of attention to design. That book makes it clear when you don't understand something it is because it is poorly designed—not because you aren't smart. Since then, I'm obsessed with how products are designed.

4. *What's a book you always recommend?*
I recently read *High Output Management* by Andy Grove. There are a lot of books written about how to be a better CEO by people who

aren't CEOs. He was CEO of Intel for more than 30 years. It's a how-to book about how to be a manager. It's so well thought out; it's about exactly the problems people have. For example, if you are doing a performance review, give people what you want to talk about in writing before, during, and after your meeting.

5. *What's a strategy to keep focused?*

   I try to break everything into small tasks. I'm not good at doing things that take months, but I am good at doing things that take a half an hour. I break things down into 15- and 30-minute pieces.

6. *When you were a kid, what did you want to be when you grew up?*

   At first, my mother was very concerned because I wanted to be a fire truck—not a firefighter. Then I wanted to be a policeman, a doctor, an astronomer, and then I settled on professor, which I ended up being for the first part of my career. I think a lot of it had to do with TV. I watched TV shows with a policeman, and it seemed cool. I was a big fan of the show *ER*, and I thought that's what I wanted to be.

7. *What did you learn from the worst boss you ever had?*

I don't think I've really had a boss. When I started leading a team, I would micromanage everything they were doing because I wanted it just so. Over time, I have learned to bite my tongue in meetings and that I should only speak up if I feel extremely strongly about something. People who report to me have gotten better at their jobs, because they have more responsibility and learn from their mistakes.

8. *Who has influenced you most when it comes to how you approach your work?*

I got a Ph.D. in computer science, and I had an awesome advisor, Manuel Blum. He won the Turing Award, which is basically the equivalent of the Nobel Prize for computer science. I learned so much from this guy; he was just so humble and thought about everything so deeply.

I spend most of my weekends thinking about things that other people might not think much about, but I think about them over and over again. It's kind of obsessive, but from that, a lot of good stuff really comes out.

9. *What's a trip that changed you?*

I grew up in Guatemala. The first time I came to the U.S. really changed me. The first thing I thought was, "This is where I want to live." I know a lot of countries are more orderly, but at the time, Guatemala was extremely chaotic. Everything in the U.S. was so orderly. People stood in line and used turn signals. That such a society could exist was amazing. For many people, that's not surprising, but for me, that was surprising.

10. *What inspires you?*

That has changed over time. At first, what inspired me was to work on hard technological problems. I didn't particularly care about the impact; I just wanted to solve difficult problems. Now, the main thing that inspires me is the impact something can have. With Duolingo, what inspires me is our mission: trying to give people language education.

11. *What was your first business idea, and what did you do with it?*

I had what I thought was a pretty serious business idea when I was about 12. I also thought I was the first person to have this idea, and I thought it was a great idea.

Neither of those were true. The idea was to see if you could generate electricity through motion.

I thought this would allow us to make gyms for free. Connect the exercise equipment to the power grid. Anyone who is exercising would be generating electricity, and I would be able to sell that electricity to the power company. Therefore, I don't have to charge anyone to come and exercise. My gym would be free, and everybody else's gym would be expensive, so I would be able to take over the gym world.

It turns out this is a pretty common bad idea. The reason it doesn't work is because humans are pretty crappy at generating electricity. The amount of electricity you could generate this way is worth nothing. There is an even bigger problem. Gyms make their money from people who don't show up, and for this idea, you need people to show up.

12. *What was an early job that taught you something important or useful that you still use today?*

I started this company called reCAPTCHA. It was acquired by Google, and I spent some time at Google after the acquisition. I didn't know it at the time, but it was extremely impactful. I really learned how a well-run company operates. By just being there, I was able to see how they did things, and I applied a lot of it to Duolingo.

13. *What's the best advice you ever took?*

I was complaining that I didn't want to give a talk that I had promised to do. Colleagues said to me, "With things like talks, you usually get asked to do them a year in advance." The advice was, if you are ever invited to do something six months or more in advance, ask yourself if you would want to do this if it was next week. If it's no, you should just decline.

14. *What's the worst piece of advice you ever got?*

I don't know if it's bad universally, or if it was just bad for me. When you're building a product, the typical advice is to listen to what your users are saying. I have found that is terrible advice for Duolingo. The spirit of the advice is good, but a lot of times, there is a problem that arises. If the feedback channels are such that only a few users get to talk to you, you are only hearing the loudest ones, not all of them, and that is where it breaks down.

We have a forum on our website where people can talk about language, but they often ask about features. I have found that listening to people in the forums is a terrible idea. For example, we redesigned the website a few years ago, and people in the forum were saying how terrible it was. Hundreds of posts about how this was the worst decision we had ever made. All the while, we were looking at the metrics for the new website, and they were significantly better.

If you are just listening to the people who reach out to you, that is a biased sample of people who are a loud minority. Of course, that is not always the case, but unless you know what you are doing, you should watch out for that bias.

15. *What's a productivity tip you swear by?*

I like my exercise routine because it's time-efficient. I just run like crazy for 15 or 16 minutes. I feel dead afterward, but at least it saves me time.

16. *Is there an app or tool you use to get things done or stay on track?*

I use [the digital workplace] Slack a lot. It helps me easily communicate with the

Duolingo team and keep track of what the team is working on day to day.

17. *What does work-life balance mean to you?*

I don't understand the meaning of that. I don't burn out because my work is my hobby. I do this because it's what I love to do. That's not a big issue for me.

18. *How do you prevent burnout?*

I guess I am a workaholic, but I have learned to cap the number of hours a day that I spend working. My biggest strategy is no matter what I am doing, at around 8 p.m., I stop working.

19. *When you're faced with a creativity block, what's your strategy to get innovating?*

This happens often, and I have learned over time is to just let time pass. Do something else—that really helps.

20. *What are you learning now?*

It is kind of a shameless plug, but I'm learning Portuguese on Duolingo. It's close to Spanish, and I'm a native Spanish speaker. I'm very bad at learning languages, which is pretty funny, but on this one, I'm making some progress.

LEADING TO SUCCESS—
REFLECTIONS

Can you become a transformational leader? Can you admit and acknowledge your own mistakes? Can you accept and use feedback? Trust your instincts once in a while? Delegate? Stay focused as Luis von Ahn does by breaking things down into smaller pieces? These are just some of the many possible factors that can help you hone your skills as a transformational leader.

Leadership, however, also means having the right tools in place, yet not every leadership style will require you to use every tool in your toolbox. For example, your delegating skills may be quite limited when there are only two of you running the entire business, and you may not be able to follow your instincts when working with scientists who are using formulas that feature dangerous chemicals. The point is: not every leader will use all the approaches, steps, or suggestions mentioned in the previous pages. But in many cases, it's worthwhile to have as many tools as possible should you be afforded the opportunity to use them.

Often, you will find that your style of leadership will change based on the people, the teams, or the projects you are leading.

A more aggressive style may motivate the research and development group, while marketing may work best when left to be autocratic and work on their own. The creative department, on the other hand, may need more ongoing support. Successful leadership often means knowing the people you are leading and understanding what makes them tick as teams and as individuals.

There are some across-the-board leadership traits, however, that you will almost always need when leading to success, including trust, determination, people skills, and the ability to communicate well, which includes being able to listen.

As you set out on your path to success as a leader, you may want to hook your impending star to leaders that best align with who you are and with what you believe. Study the methodology of the leaders you would most want to emulate. Examine what they did to become successful. What were the results, and what did the people they led have to say about their leadership? The most famous leaders are not necessarily the people who made the most money, but those who inspired the most people.

The previous articles and the books mentioned in Chapter 23, along with new leadership books, articles, and blogs being released daily present many inspiring road maps set forth by successful leaders. From the many perspectives of the writers included, as well as their stories, you can glean the attributes, strategies, steps, qualities, and styles of leadership that will put you on the path to success. Study and learn how to be an intentional leader, while honing your skills—and remember that leadership is not about you, it's about being "other centered." As Seth Godin said, "Leadership is the art of giving people a platform for spreading ideas that work."

RESOURCES

(In Order of Appearance)

Thank you to our talented Entrepreneur contributors whose content is featured in this book. For more information about these contributors, including author bios, visit us at www.entrepreneur.com.

1. Adam Bornstein and Jordan Bornstein, "22 Qualities That Make a Great Leader," *Entrepreneur*, October 28, 2016, www. entrepreneur.com/slideshow/299443.

2. Sherrie Campbell, "Seven Traits of Exceptional Leaders," *Entrepreneur*, March 23, 2017, www.entrepreneur.com/article/290967.

3. Elinor Stutz, this article originally appeared under the title "How to Detect a Leader vs. a Follower," *Entrepreneur*, March 4, 2017, www.entrepreneur.com/article/290026.

4. Nicolas Cole, this article originally appeared under the title "9 Ways to Recognize a Real Leader," *Entrepreneur*, March 19, 2017, www.entrepreneur.com/article/286367.

5. Gwen Moran, this article originally appeared under the title "5 Keys to Inspiring Leadership, No Matter Your Style," *Entrepreneur*, June 14, 2013, www.entrepreneur.com/article/227012.

6. Tor Constantino, this article originally appeared under the title "5 Attributes of the Super Successful," *Entrepreneur*, March 30, 2017, www.entrepreneur.com/article/292120.

7. Tom Gimbel, this article originally appeared under the title "4 Things the New Leader of an Organization Should Do Right Away," *Entrepreneur*, March 22, 2017, www.entrepreneur.com/article/290876.

8. William Hall, this article originally appeared under the title "4 Steps to Build Strategically Critical Leadership-Development Programs," *Entrepreneur*, April 4, 2017, www.entrepreneur.com/article/290487.

9. Gordon Tredgold, this article originally appeared under the title "6 Mistakes That Rookie Leaders Make Which Can Cause Them To Fail," *Entrepreneur*, February 23, 2017, www.entrepreneur.com/article/288150.

10. Rehan Ijaz, this article originally appeared under the title "3 Strategies for Projecting Success and Confidence as a Leader," *Entrepreneur*, March 19, 2017, www.entrepreneur.com/article/286363.

11. Steffen Maier, this article originally appeared under the title "6 Changes Your Company Must Make to Develop More Female Leaders," *Entrepreneur*, March 2, 2017, www.entrepreneur.com/article/289632.

12. Anna Johansson, this article originally appeared under the title "4 Ways a Follower Can Become a Leader," *Entrepreneur*, April 20, 2017, www.entrepreneur.com/article/274345.

13. Todd Wolfenbarger, "Why Leaders Should View Themselves as Servants," *Entrepreneur*,

March 25, 2017, www.entrepreneur.com/article/285837.

14. Gene Marks, this article originally appeared under the title "That Time Bill Gates Answered a Tech Support Call ... and Crushed It," *Entrepreneur*, March 1, 2017, www.entrepreneur.com/article/289857.

15. Sherrie Campbell, this article originally appeared under the title "8 Ways to Advocate for Your Team's Success," *Entrepreneur*, February 23, 2017, www.entrepreneur.com/article/289583.

16. Heather R. Huhman, this article originally appeared under the title "5 Things the Best Leaders Do Every Day," *Entrepreneur*, January 30, 2017, www.entrepreneur.com/article/288242.

17. Calvin Wayman, this article originally appeared under the title "4 Ways to Reinvent Yourself After Hitting Rock Bottom," *Entrepreneur*, April 5, 2017, www.entrepreneur.com/article/282404.

18. Jennifer Biry, "How to Motivate Your Team Members by Putting Their Needs First," *Entrepreneur*, February 20, 2017, www.entrepreneur.com/article/289365.

19. Matt Mayberry, this article originally appeared under the title "How 1 Executive Became a

Transformational Leader," *Entrepreneur*, March 14, 2017, www.entrepreneur.com/article/290414.

20. Heather R. Huhman, this article originally appeared under the title "Being a Trusted Leader: What You Need to Know As Your Company Grows," *Entrepreneur*, March 14, 2017, www.entrepreneur.com/article/290440.

21. Jeffrey Hayzlett, this article originally appeared under the title "5 Leadership Lessons on the Court, for Business off the Court," *Entrepreneur*, March 15, 2017, www.entrepreneur.com/article/290491.

22. Robert Glazer, this article originally appeared under the title "How to Lead Versus Manage, to Improve Your Team's Success," *Entrepreneur*, March 11, 2017, www.entrepreneur.com/article/282051.

23. Deep Patel, this article originally appeared under the title "10 Books Every Leader Should Read to Be Successful," *Entrepreneur*, February 19, 2017, www.entrepreneur.com/article/287517.

24. Jayson DeMers, "Should You Take Business Advice That Contradicts Your Instincts," *Entrepreneur*, March 2, 2017, www.entrepreneur.com/article/289687.

25 Nina Zipkin, this article originally appeared under the title "Why This Founder Says the Worst Advice He Ever Got Was to Listen to His Users," *Entrepreneur*, March 16, 2017, www. entrepreneur.com/article/290664.

Reader's Notes

Reader's Notes

_____

_____

_____

_____

_____

_____

_____

_____

_____

_____

_____

_____

_____

_____

_____

_____

_____

Reader's Notes

_____

_____

_____

_____

_____

_____

_____

_____

_____

_____

_____

_____

_____

_____

_____

_____

_____

Reader's Notes

_____

_____

_____

_____

_____

_____

_____

_____

_____

_____

_____

_____

_____

_____

_____

_____